D0415757

Macmillan Building and Surveying Series

Macmillan Building and Surveying Series
Series Standing Order ISBN 0–333-69333–7

You can receive future titles in this series as they are published by placing a standing order. Please contact your bookseller or, in the case of difficulty, write to us at the address below with your name and address, the title of the series and the ISBN quoted above.

Customer Services Department, Macmillan Distribution Ltd
Houndmills, Basingstoke, Hampshire, RG21 6XS, England.

Facilities Management

An Explanation

Second Edition

Alan Park

FRICS, MCIOB, ACIArb., FBIFM, MaPS
Managing Director, Stride Project Management Ltd
Director, Stride Treglown Ltd
Facilities Manager, Stride FM
Planning Supervisor

MACMILLAN

First edition 1994
Reprinted twice
Second edition 1998

Published 1998 by
MACMILLAN PRESS LTD
Houndmills, Basingstoke, Hampshire RG21 6XS
and London
Companies and representatives
throughout the world

ISBN 0–333–73798–9

A catalogue record for this book is available
from the British Library.

This book is printed on paper suitable for recycling and
made from fully managed and sustained forest resources.

10 9 8 7 6 5 4 3 2 1
07 06 05 04 03 02 01 00 99 98

Copy-edited and typeset by Povey–Edmondson
Tavistock and Rochdale, England

Printed in Great Britain by
Antony Rowe Ltd
Chippenham, Wilts

Contents

List of Figures and Examples

Figures

Examples

Foreword to the First Edition

It gives me great pleasure to write the foreword to this instructive and authoritative book on *Facilities Management* with which I have had the privilege to be associated throughout the writing of the book.

Facilities management is becoming an increasingly important area of professional activity as the management of many classes of property becomes more sophisticated and the requirements of both owners and occupiers of buildings assume greater importance, accompanied by the increasing expectations of the occupants of properties.

The development of facilities management as an operational process has been accompanied by rapid changes in computer aided techniques which have such an invaluable and far-reaching effect on the total facilities management process, as is so effectively described and illustrated in this book.

The book examines in substantial detail, yet in a succinct and masterly way, the many facets of facilities management and discusses their relevance and the operation of techniques that culminate in an efficient service to building occupiers. The text is supported throughout with excellent practical examples which will be of great value to the reader.

Alan Park is to be complimented for devoting so much time, care and skill to the writing of the book and for the enthusiasm and dedication with which he approached this quite daunting task, amidst his own professional activities in this field. His time-consuming efforts have been amply rewarded in the production of this comprehensive, yet concise, practical guide for professional advisers as an invaluable and much needed service to occupiers of property. It encompasses advice on the many interrelated aspects of space planning and costing, building maintenance management, life cycle costing, control of all operational services, including such important activities as security, cleaning and internal communications, registering and monitoring assets, health and safety, building services management, and dealing with a variety of related yet important activities.

I am confident that this book will soon become a recognised source of reference by both professionals and students alike in this rapidly developing area of activity, in which a number of professional bodies are taking an active interest and where an increasing number of universities are including it in the curriculum of building and surveying courses.

Professor Ivor H. Seeley
Series Editor
Macmillan Building and Surveying Series

Preface to the First Edition

The purpose of this book is to provide a definitive introduction to facilities management (FM) of premises.

The subject is of interest to students wishing to follow a career in FM, new recruits from other management disciplines and existing professional consultants seeking diversification in their skills.

This book seeks to stimulate the inventive thought processes necessary for facilities managers to be successful in the field. It does not therefore set out to be an in depth academic research paper as the diversity of problems to be overcome prevents this book from anticipating and addressing each and every possible event exactly, but it does contain examples and methods that can be applied universally with the minimum of adaptation to solve many tasks.

Above all it demonstrates to potential managers that FM is a mix of organised research and pre-planning together with an ability to react decisively with logic to unannounced events.

FM is a stimulating career on the threshold of professional status that will reward the ambitious with a route to the highest levels of management.

Bristol   Alan Park
Autumn 1993

Preface to the Second Edition

Progress of facilities management and its recognition as a strategic management function has necessitated this second edition of *Facilities Management*. There are two new chapters dealing with the management of the property portfolio and a series of case studies drawn from current experience plus additional material in five other chapters.

Above all, the growing awareness of environmental issues and the drive towards conservation and sustainability of resources further promotes the key importance of effective facilities management. The support of government, and international opinion, for our environment further emphasises the contribution expected from facilities management, and this book will alert practitioners to the fascinating diversity of this subject.

Bristol   Alan Park
Autumn 1997

Acknowledgements

For the opportunity to research and develop the facilities management services on which this book is based I am grateful to:

Stride Treglown Limited

and

Stride FM

The late Professor Ivor Seeley, as the Series Editor, who was a source of encouragement and advice throughout the long hours of writing the first edition.

I would also like to acknowledge my gratitude to Steve Twigg for the cover design.

Also, many thanks to Jill Sage who has wordprocessed my handwriting willingly into a usable manuscript.

Finally, to my wife Lou, daughters Caroline and Amy, for their support and understanding throughout.

1 Origins and Objectives

Anybody picking up a building or property journal could be excused for thinking that facilities management is a new profession, such is the increasing prominence that it is attracting in the technical press. The many and varied functions performed are not new, but the trend towards creating an all-embracing professional who harnesses these complementary functions together into a cohesive approach to workspace management is. The role of the facilities manager is recognised as something more pro-active than that of the traditional estates manager.

So what is facilities management? It is the structuring of building plant and contents to enhance the creation of the end product. As with all systems it is the generated benefit to the business or activity that matters, not the system itself. The end product can, in this case, be a tangible manufactured item or a service; in either case the product benefits in competitiveness and quality.

Our principal objective is to manage property and once we realise that property is a finite resource, as is the energy it consumes, the importance becomes clear. That idealism alone is not enough motivation for commercial organisations to invest in facilities management, the real driving force is one of economics. The cost of providing buildings and running them as a place of work is an overhead, however necessary, on any company, so better planned buildings, sensible use and a willingness to reorganise reduce the capital cost and the running costs. Overhead costs are controlled, and profits, cashflow and shareholders prosper; but we are also investing in the future by conserving building stock.

The following chapters of this book will deal specifically with particular aspects of the facilities manager's activities, including space planning and costing, maintenance, operational services and others. The objective is to provide and continue the best compromise between working conditions and cost.

It is imperative to get the usage of the building correct; wasted space, inefficient departmental interfaces, together with an unattractive working environment, far outweigh the popular implications of isolated rental appraisal and maintenance costs. The facilities manager's success will come from an in-depth grasp of applied economics influenced by a strong practical approach to property occupation. In our materialistic age the current theory of economics seeks to reconcile available resources to a virtually infinite desire for goods and services.

Charts 1 and 2 in Figure 1.1 are a simple demonstration of the effect of facilities management in controlling the overheads of an organisation. Bear in mind that raw materials, production labour and energy used in production are direct product costs and that conversely the property costs are not directly related to the product. The property costs are therefore an overhead; chart 1 shows a typical unmanaged overhead situation. The overhead is constant throughout the sample charging period – and the effect of declining company income is clear, with successive losses appearing that will exhaust the corporate resources and create a cashflow crisis, sooner or later. The increasing proportion of overheads to the direct costs is obvious.

A typical panic management reaction to such a situation is to make production workers redundant on the pretext of meeting production and demand. Such action further exaggerates the imbalance of overheads and direct costs making the product increasingly uncompetitive. We have memories of a deep recession and a lesson learned by the successful survivors is to reduce product cost and therefore market price to compete in the post-recession recovery.

Now look at chart 2; it shows the same income profile as chart 1 and the same direct cost, as after all, these are generated by the company's performance in the market place. The overheads have been controlled in this example and there is a profitable result on five of the eight accounting periods, even through the bottom of the market in periods 4, 5 and 6. A recovery is beginning to show in periods 7 and 8, with the company able to gear up in a controlled manner. It is a fact in our recession/boom/recession economy that more companies fail on the way out of recession than on the way in; this is usually due to the increased financial demands of stocking and gearing up in advance of sales, which push cashflow into unsupported deficit.

Continued overhead control into the boom period allows expenditure to be channelled into wealth creation and reserves.

These two examples are simplistic, but they are intended to demonstrate a principle where facilities management has a direct input into the commercial survival and prosperity of any organisation where the facilities costs can account for more than 50% of the total overhead. The introduction of facilities management to an organisation can easily

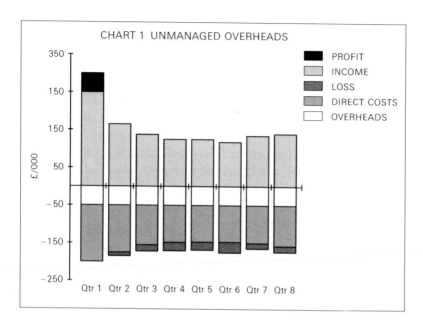

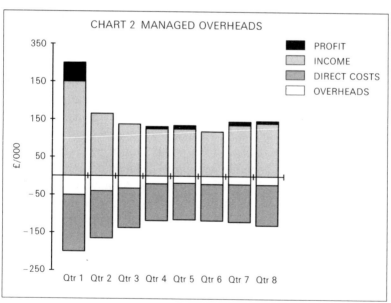

Figure 1.1   Unmanaged and managed overheads

effect a 10% reduction in workspace costs, with twice that figure as a realistic target in the medium term. That would equate to a minimum 5% to 10% saving in the total company overhead. The pie chart in Figure 3.1 (chapter 3) indicates graphically the components used to calculate the workspace costs.

References so far have been to companies, products and services, but these economic principles and the business objectives apply to any organisation that receives funding through income, grants or proceeds of sales and needs to balance that income with its expenditure.

The most beneficial cost controlling activities within facilities management are:

- Space planning and costing.
- Asset tracking.
- Maintenance.
- Life cycle costing.

The space planning function seeks to match available and future planned space in type and form to match needs. The space function, using the response and power of personal computer (PC) graphics, is described in chapters 2 and 3, covering the application of computer aided design (CAD) that develops into computer aided facilities management (CAFM), linking CAD drawings with integrated databases.

Asset tracking may not be instantly recognisable as an activity, but it is a logical development and replacement of traditional inventories. Companies dependent on external funding of working capital through banks, venture capitalists or shareholders are deeply interested in the net asset valuation of their worth; it is the basis of much bank-based financial support and, together with profit/dividend potential earnings, sets the level of share value in a floating market. A strong net asset value gives confidence in long-term stability which, together with a strong share value, presents one of the least costly funding routes for raising development or expansion capital.

A company with shares trading at the top end of its range will not be commercially damaged by a rights issue to raise capital; the share value will reduce but, given continuous good management, will rise again. The company will then be able to invest with only the liability of paying dividends to the increased share allocation and not the burden of interest on bank borrowing. Bank borrowing has unfortunate side effects; it passes some control over the business outside where trading may not be fully understood and it adversely affects the net asset value of the company. Chapter 6 looks at assets, their registers and tracking in detail.

Maintenance and life cycle costing are interrelated with maintenance planning, which is often thought to be the facilities manager's principal task. Reality is not quite the same, for in fact the facilities manager's task, if properly developed, covers a wide range of activities relating to the provision and use of buildings and contents. Maintenance is reviewed in chapter 4 with references to total quality management (TQM) and quality assurance (QA). Life cycle costing (covered in chapter 7) examines the balance of cost against life expectancy.

Facilities management (FM) is not just about controlling cost; there are several significant services that can be managed through FM systems to ensure the smooth operation of a company or organisation. These services are:

- Health and safety monitoring.
- Component specifications.
- Systems and software.
- Services.

All these are examined in detail in the appropriate chapters that follow.

Property is a finite resource that needs to repay the capital cost of its creation on an investment basis. Those buildings that serve a public need but cannot satisfy the investment return principle can only be funded with grant, government or other non-commercial assistance. Buildings have a value cycle whereby they are developed to satisfy current and perceived future demand. If the developer makes the correct judgement the building will grow in investment value, driven by demand. Progress, however, changes demand and in time most buildings will have matured to their peak value and will slip into decline. The application of active facilities management that studies the use of the building and adjusts it and the occupation to best match current demands will slow the value decline. Refurbishment, alteration and even change of use all prolong the life of the building. Most cities have easily recognisable examples of fine architectural buildings that have changed use – Victorian railway stations into retail use, and churches into offices. This all helps to preserve heritage, as well as conserve building stock.

Some buildings will have a defined lifespan and will be constructed accordingly; here the facilities manager's task is different. In this case the objective is to extract the maximum benefit from the property over its planned life, without incurring excessive cost in keeping it running towards the end of the period. The chapter on life cycle costing is very relevant to any managers in this position. The ultimate conclusion for any building at the end of its economic life is demolition, which then releases a site for new development, thus starting the cycle over again.

The facilities manager, while dealing with day-to-day occupational demands, has a long-term influence on property economics.

References throughout this book to buildings, premises or property does not restrict the management role to conventional enclosed structures. The real activity concerns the use of space, whether it be buildings, civil engineering structures or even open space like construction and storage yards. The management can be on a two-dimensional form, or three-dimensional, considering for example floor plan layouts in the former case, through to fully integrated studies for installations like services and cable networks in the latter case.

The economic benefits of facilities management show through improved productivity, better product quality and overhead control. The control of overheads generates a return to the organisation year after year, but engaging a full-time facilities manager or even setting up a department adds directly to the overhead. It is important therefore to ensure that the financial benefits more than justify the cost of a full-time, in-house service.

This does not mean that the activities described in this book are the exclusive property of large organisations with extensive estates. This activity need not be a full-time commitment for the employee, but caution is needed here to give the facilities management role the importance that it deserves in order to run effectively.

The use of a professional facilities management consultant can solve these problems by supporting an over-stretched in-house manager on specific projects like market testing outsourced support services, or for system development, in order to add more management functions or update records and technology.

The profession of facilities management is gaining respectability through the interest of various professional bodies and educational establishments. The Chartered Institute of Building is developing examination standards, the Royal Institution of Chartered Surveyors has a skills panel on the subject and there are bodies like the British Institute of Facilities Management formed out of the amalgamation of the Association of Facilities Managers with the Institute of Facilities Managers where membership leads to an interchange of current views.

The most encouraging sign that this is evolving into a recognised professional discipline must be the creation of structured study and examinations leading to degrees and corporate membership of chartered bodies like the CIOB.

2 Space Planning

2.1 Visual indexing

Facilities management is all about collecting and interpreting data on diverse facets of property use. Computer databases are the ideal vehicles in which to log, store and manipulate data; almost unlimited information can be measured and entered en masse. Simple databases operate very satisfactorily as stand-alone software, where a limited range of services are monitored. The strength of such information storage is its capacity for expansion and the diversity of subject. This strength is a time bomb that sooner or later destroys the effectiveness of a database as an FM tool; it becomes large and requires greater and greater operator familiarity with its structure in order to interrogate successfully.

The answer to the problem in property terms is visual indexing. Line managers responsible for estate and facilities management will always be familiar with the physical layout of their buildings, so why not use estate and building plans as the index.

Again, in simple application a site or building plan pinned on the wall with database access codes written on by hand provides a quick and easy reference trail to the appropriate information. A bound volume of A3 or A4 drawings of all floor plans serves as the database handbook for larger systems.

As the use of the system grows, managers are tempted by the database flexibility to add further levels of information and soon the limitations of the hard copy indexes becomes a frustration. Who wants a system that allows easy logging of multi-level information but requires physical amendment of the index?

Apart from the time-consuming irritation, the human element leads to mistakes, particularly under pressure.

The ultimate solution is to computer-base the entire operation, and this is best achieved in the author's experience in the following way.

First, a fundamental rethink of the system hierarchy, to make the database generation subservient to the visual index plans, is the route to success.

The building user decides which aspects he wishes to manage — space planning, the subject of this chapter, is one such activity — and codes a computer-generated plan with the database code. Industry-standard CAD systems are ideal for this purpose; the author's particular experience is with AutoCAD, where attributes planted on the drawing serve as the database link.

The attribute is primed with basic information generated on the drawing; in the case of space planning it is a good idea to include a room or compartment area space use reference and the room number. This identifies the space accurately. The attribute generates the database by interfacing with standard database software.

So now we have a drawing that has generated a database to show the first three fields of area, use and location.

Once into the database further fields of information can be added at will, without cluttering the index drawing; the data can be re-arranged, interrogated and relevant extracts can be printed out.

Preserving the system hierarchy is the only convention to be guarded. The fields generated by the drawing can only be altered on the drawing, to do so directly on the database will corrupt the system.

In practice, the manager uses a PC to store the drawings and data-bases; the access trail first displays a location plan of the entire estate, whether it be one building or many. A typical display resembles that in Figure 2.1. The manager's familiarity with the layout allows him to pick the area of interest and zoom in until the attributes are identifiable, as in Figure 2.2. Picking the attribute AAG024 directly accesses the database at the precise point to generate a screen display like Figure 2.3.

The database may now be driven to arrange itself to conform with the manager's particular requirement. It could, for example, display all areas of the estate in similar use by ascending or descending area. The manipulation of databases is covered later in chapter 8.

2.2   Active space modelling

Ask any building users or company finance directors if they use their premises efficiently and all will have opinions. These opinions are all too often subjective, based on comments like 'when I walk round the office it's full of people, paper and activity' or 'we could really do with more space'; such responses are not very scientific; they are more of a gut

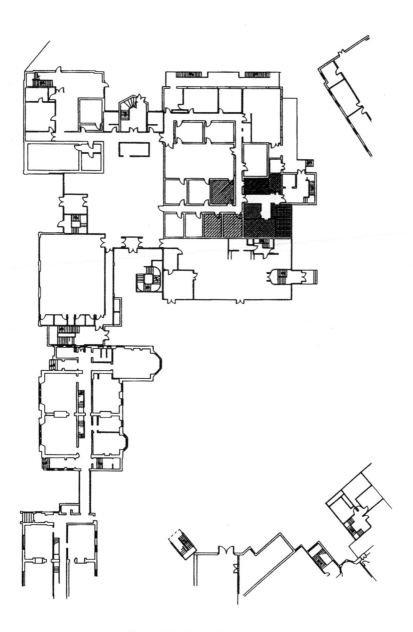

Figure 2.1   Estate location plan

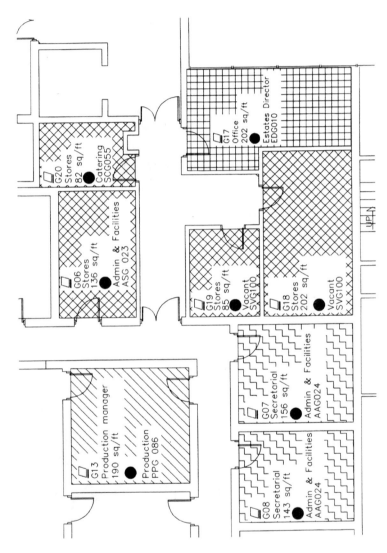

Figure 2.2   Floorspace allocation plan

SPACE ALLOCATION : EXTRACT REPORT						datapoint Aug-93	
room no	usage	use type	cost centre	area sf	area sm	rate £/sm	cost allocated
G06	Admin & Facilities	S	ASG023	136	12.63	72.00	909.36
G07	Admin & Facilities	A	AAG024	156	14.49	118.00	1709.82
G08 **	Admin & Facilities	A	AAG024	143	13.29	118.00	1568.22
G13 **	Production	P	PPG086	190	17.65	135.00	2382.75
G17 **	Estates Director	D	EDG010	202	18.77	155.00	2909.35
G18	Stores	V	SVG100	202	18.77	72.00	1351.44
G19	Stores	V	SVG100	85	7.90	72.00	568.80
G20 **	Stores	C	SCG055	82	7.62	85.00	647.70

Figure 2.3   Space allocation: extract report

feeling response and not really good enough in our highly competitive world. Always remember that premises are overheads in commercial and industrial applications; they cost money and do not by their mere existence generate any wealth. One lesson learnt so well following the decline of the 1980s boom is that survival and ensuing prosperity depend on overhead control, with the maximum investment chan-nelled into production.

One of the most important strategies in business today is that of providing space for the businesses to function. A conflict exists in that buildings are resources that take time to create and need extended periods of use to justify the investment. The need for built space is volatile by comparison, reacting to market pressures and the success rate of the business. Unfortunately, the two sides of the equation react badly to each other. In expansionist times space is at a premium and therefore expensive, whereas in recession there is surplus space at bargain prices but little opportunity for businesses to take advantage.

The answer to this dilemma is active space modelling within the space planning regime that allows the flow of activity within the space to be planned and applied to the design of new buildings or even the layout of existing buildings. This activity lends itself to CAD applications, taking full advantage of the computer's ability to accept an educated trial and error approach, the 'what if?' concept of refining the solution.

New buildings offer the greatest success here if the design can be influenced throughout the pre-construction phase of procurement. Do not, however, assume that, once the design is fixed or the building built, active space modelling is redundant. Its scope may be inhibited, but unless the ideal arrangement is established through CAD modelling, the degree of compromise in occupying an established building remains unquantified. Often alterations can be introduced to reduce the penalty of unsympathetic design. The choice will as always be one of economics.

2.3   Existing and new buildings

A prospective building user is confronted with a choice, should he develop a new building or occupy existing stock? This choice is a distillation of many considerations; does the use dictate a bespoke design, how urgent is the timescale to operational level location, site availability, funding, grants and many more considerations.

The decision is easy if one consideration has overriding importance; in most cases the choice is made on the bottom line cost.

Many a wrong decision has been made in this way through ignorance of the true cost implications of one building compared with another. How many bottom line decisions take proper account of the less obvious property costs? We can all think immediately of the obvious ones – rent/finance charges, rates and service charges. What about maintenance, insurance, energy costs, relocation expenses, staff welfare, availability of labour?

It is the skill of the facilities manager that researches and arranges the data on all these points into an understandable format and allows senior management to make long-term property decisions with full knowledge rather than in partial ignorance.

The integrity of the FM data must be beyond dispute, particularly if it points towards a building solution with higher obvious costs where the decisive benefits are to be found in less apparent efficiencies like increased productivity. There are always self-appointed critics to be silenced.

2.4   Trial layouts

The goal in building occupancy is to achieve the perfect layout to suit the activity to be performed in the building, both now and at any time in the future. That is a definition of perfection and is impossible, but FM is about getting closer and closer to that goal.

When planning occupancy the user sets out the ideal operation with attention to production flow.

Production flow does not just apply to manufacturing process, it is also the continuity of operation between people, equipment, processes and departments. It is just as important in offices, warehouses, retail stores, hospitals, schools – in fact in any building where people congregate with a common purpose.

Departmental requirements are set through consultation, questionnaires and past experience. Once this data is assembled it must be vetted for realism; there is no point in allowing managers to demand space which when totalled exceeds the area available for allocation. This is a common problem that can be resolved in two ways; either senior management makes the ultimate decisions, or a period of broking and negotiation between managers arrives at a compromise. The latter is the best approach and the threat of the former will prevent the negotiations from becoming protracted.

This occupational space data can be recoded manually in single projects but once the plan form or size becomes complicated a computer database becomes essential. Now we have the added benefit of the interface between CAD and this database.

The working environment is an essential part of departmental efficiency and the example illustrated in Figure 2.4 shows the space hatching corresponding to departmental use. If we assume in this office example that there are areas occupied for common services, accounts, toilets and kitchens together with circulation, we can begin to analyse the conflicting space requirements into a series of trial layouts. The layout in Figure 2.4 supports a working relationship of sorts between common services and accounts but leaves these departments fragmented. In this simplistic example a second trial layout as in Figure 2.5 creates a much more efficient relationship between the departments, with reduced travel distances. The human factor benefits from increased contact; nothing causes more friction than isolation.

The mechanics of trial layouts are not new; the real advance is the use of computers to run CAD and databases with such ease that trial

16

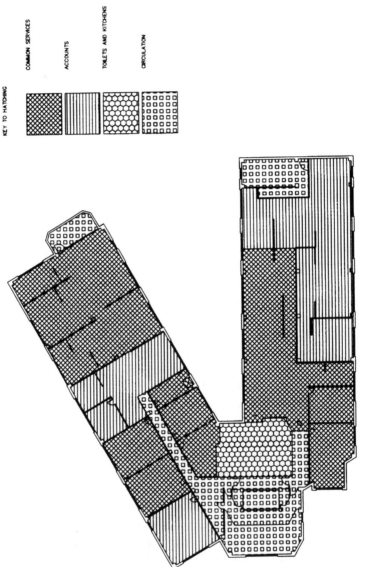

KEY TO HATCHING

COMMON SERVICES

ACCOUNTS

TOILETS AND KITCHENS

CIRCULATION

Figure 2.4   Departmental space use: fragmented

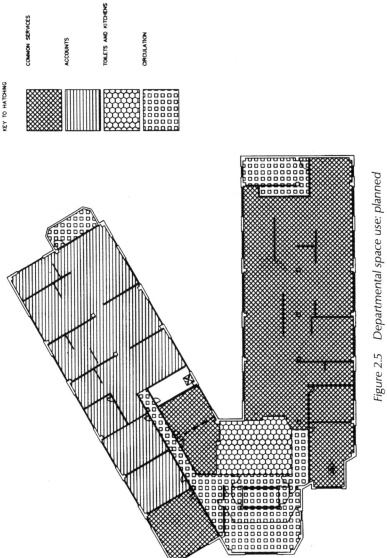

KEY TO HATCHING

COMMON SERVICES

ACCOUNTS

TOILETS AND KITCHENS

CIRCULATION

Figure 2.5 Departmental space use: planned

and error solutions can be tested on the 'what if?' principle. There is no substitute for a skilled designer in these situations, but if we are armed with the capability to test a range of solutions graphically, the final outcome pursues our goal of perfection. The space database driven by the CAD-generated solutions can be regularly interrogated to ensure that the agreed space allocations are being honoured.

2.5   Estate development plans

There is a bigger picture to address for those space users that occupy complete estates at one or more locations. Before space planning is conducted for individual buildings, allocation within the estate needs to be planned. This planning is carried out using CAD programmes but bearing in mind the added considerations of future demand, rationalisation and disposal of surplus space.

Estate development plans address the strategic planning issues before individual buildings are space modelled.

3 Space Planning Data in Cost Control

3.1 Workspace cost

This activity is the cornerstone of facilities management, creating a management tool that uses the data available from the space planning exercises and converting it into a financial control procedure. The creation of the space planning data described in chapter 2 serves a primary function; it arranges the physical occupation of the building into the best compromise, but the cost of providing workspace so arranged is the final adjudicator.

If we now treat the same building, whether built or not, as an existing space with the occupation arrangements defined, it becomes necessary to research the overall cost of providing every square metre.

The obvious directly related costs spring to mind; rent or an equivalent annualised capital cost and rates are easy as they are based on floor area and are largely constant in cashflow terms. Other costs are more obscure, like those for energy, service operations including cleaning, maintenance and safety. These are more difficult to quantify on an annual basis and also the spend pattern throughout the year is not constant, being affected by seasonal and operational factors.

Insurance in any occupier's overheads contains a large element directly linked to the building; there is fabric cover plus accidental damage and environmental factors that can be related back to building type, construction and location.

If maintenance accounts for general wear and tear, more major items identified by life cycle analysis, ranging from major component renewal, lifts, boilers and the like to the entire refurbishment/replacement of the building, need to be funded, perhaps even through an advance sinking fund.

All these items relate to the space but, in order to be meaningful, are best allocated over the workspace areas rather than gross or even landlord-type, net lettable areas.

So, what is workspace area? In a mixed manufacturing and administrative office development it is not just the shop floor, it is the total of all areas occupied by personnel and equipment directly engaged in the function of the business.

Computer suites, post rooms, offices, manufacturing areas, warehousing for example, are all included, whereas circulation, both landlord's and internal, is not.

If in doubt ask the question of any space – is it occupied by anything or anyone directly engaged in the business – answer 'yes' to be included, 'no' to be excluded.

The total cost can now be divided by this workspace area and the results can easily show that the cost of housing the active parts of the business is the rent times a factor of between 3 and 7, even higher in specialist occupations.

This is therefore the level of expenditure that the facilities management programme needs to evaluate, control and report to higher management. It is common to hear building occupiers worrying about rental levels, particularly during the lead up to review points. The facilities manager armed with workspace costs can quickly add perspective by finding economies through efficiency in the overall costs that often totally negate rent review increases.

The chart in Figure 3.1 is a simplified analysis of the workspace costs of an office building and shows that the rent is 32% of the overall cost, representing a factor of 3.125. Most of the segments on the chart are data from obvious sources like rates and energy consumption costs; those of servicing, circulation, surplus space and furnishing need some explanation.

Servicing is the collective cost centre that monitors cleaning, maintenance, and specialist activities like inspection of fire extinguishers; it is in fact all the support service costs incurred in making the building comfortable to occupy.

Circulation in this example is not to be confused with landlord's circulation; it is not entrances, stairs and communal areas, but is the space necessary within any occupation required to allow free movement by people, materials and products in the course of each business activity. The best illustration of this definition is to take a typical office block let on a floor by floor basis to several tenants: on entering the building the entrance areas, stairs, lifts and landings are the landlord's circulation and lie outside the lettable floor areas, but once into the office areas rent applies. Within the offices it is necessary to plan the

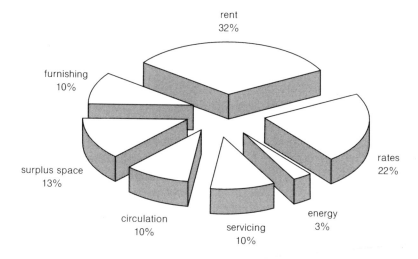

Figure 3.1   Pie chart: workspace costs

layout to achieve efficient working and that will of necessity include space for movement, space between desks and departments, space for storage and tea points. All this space is not directly productive and is analysed out into this segment which in the example represents 10% of the costs.

It must be assumed that the circulation space analysis is based upon an efficient layout that is neither over-generous, nor sub-standard, in its allocation to the occupants. In use, however, this level of efficiency is seldom achieved and, even when it is, it tends to deteriorate with time. The old adage of work expanding to fill available time can be paralleled in occupation patterns. People will occupy all the space made available to them through untidiness or territorial ambitions.

An objective reappraisal of occupational layouts can easily demonstrate large amounts of wasted space and this is categorised as surplus in the example. The chapter on space planning covers this point under active space modelling.

This chapter opened on an apparent pretext that the space planning reviews had achieved the best occupation compromise, but this cannot be so until that solution is costed. Analysis of data on other buildings allows the facilities manager to judge if the costs thrown up by the solution are competitive, and after all, business survives on its competitiveness. Here we now have the ultimate point of balance where the best space planning solution and its workspace costs are tested. If the cost is too high in relation to the business competitors, then a structured review follows with the target cost to be achieved defined.

The first action is not to attack the space planners, as after all they have already been through the give-and-take process to arrive at the best solution; the task is to scrutinise the workspace costs, looking at those elements directly controlled by the business.

An energy audit may raise recommendations for capital expenditure, but if these are more than funded by the cost benefit it will improve the workspace costs, as the overall annualised cost effect will be showing a reduction on the energy sector of the workspace costs.

Maintenance, service operations, insurance and life cycle funds are at least partly within the judgement of the occupier.

At this point the most competitive workspace costs are now established which will fall within the overall cost target.

It can be argued that the facilities management task is now a success, having achieved the best operating conditions within an acceptable controlled cost. Facilities management is not, however, a one-off exercise but is an evolving strategy. The use of buildings does not remain static, technology changes, products change, businesses respond to the market place and the facilities managers must continually monitor and apply corrective action whenever trends appear that will take the operations in the building outside predetermined tolerances.

What does this mean? We have a space planning solution and a workspace cost. The cost is worked up into a series of budgets, an overall budget with sub-budgets for each of the cost centres of rent, rates, energy, service operations – in fact all the headings used to calculate the workspace cost. The budget and sub-budgets are cashflowed, taking account of variables like seasonal influences to create a cost control platform like the one in Figure 3.2.

Actual costs as they are incurred are logged, usually by coding invoices and payments within the business's accounts department, to the relevant sub-budget, and the variance against the predefined cost control platform is calculated.

As with all budgeting, it is not a precise calculation, so some variance will be acceptable, but tolerances should be set to trigger investigation whenever the actual costs exceed that deviation either over or under the platform.

Earlier cost accounting procedures have tended to concentrate on overspending and while that is often an instant problem, facilities

PROPERTY BUDGET CASHFLOW

	rent c/flow £	rates c/flow £	energy c/flow £	serv ops c/flow £	total c/flow £
Budget					
1994					
Jan		14784	3040	8560	26384
Feb		0	2856	7780	10636
Mar	62500	0	2890	6790	72180
Apr		17768	500	4978	23246
May		17768	1584	5980	25332
Jun	62500	17768	686	4978	85932
Jul		17768	760	4567	23095
Aug		17768	500	6028	22646
Sept	62500	17768	986	6028	87282
Oct		17768	2238	7580	27586
Nov		17768	2651	8341	28760
Dec	62500	17768	3514	9088	92870
TOTAL	**250000**	**174696**	**22205**	**79048**	**525949**

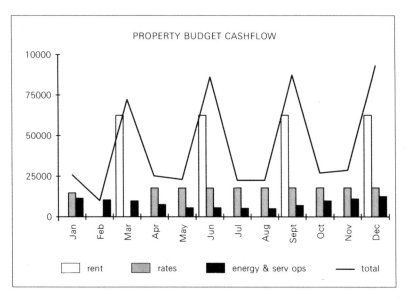

Figure 3.2   Property budget cashflow

managers understand that underspending can conceal longer-term problems of cost and safety.

All cost variances on or above the allowed tolerance must be looked into and here any trends will become apparent.

Trends are the easiest to review, particularly when they can be related to a management decision; overspend, and variances caused by a multitude of unrelated costs, are more difficult to correct and usually point to defective budgeting.

The facilities manager needs to be proactive in proposing a management review with the operational problems identified, together with solutions. Remember that the finance department will know that there is a cost problem as they will be producing the variance reports, but they will not know the cause and the options available. -

The rule in effective costing is:

- Relate cost to function.
- Establish budgets.
- Set budget tolerances.
- Monitor variances.
- Look for trends.
- Be proactive.

Cashflow variables are in many cases the application of common sense. Heating costs will obviously be higher in winter but in air conditioned buildings plant running costs can be high in summer. Solar gain is an example where proactive facilities management can lower the workspace cost.

Shading, blinds, planting, plus the introduction of natural ventilation, all help to reduce cooling plant loads with an overall cost–benefit over medium and long term occupation.

It is not just seasonal weather variables that affect the cashflow, many businesses have seasonally driven demand on their production and here the facilities manager has a valuable contribution to make towards the overall efficiency of the business.

Some businesses in manufacturing work most cost effectively on the just-in-time principle where the stock of raw materials and finished products is kept to a minimum. This is obviously important where material and therefore product costs are high and excessive stocks will tax the business's reserves. The facilities manager in this case cannot afford any unscheduled break in production as there is no stockholding buffer. Storage and warehousing is kept to a minimum, acting only as materials reception and product despatch. This type of operation is very susceptible to demand variations, so the building and its processes must be capable of rapid response, especially shutdown.

3.2   Controlling location-related cost

Most property costs are related to the space used and there are some costs within the business's overheads that can be allocated to particular locations in the buildings. The point of this exercise is to create a monitoring and control process to highlight excesses.

We all understand the space-related costs like rent and rates whether they be controlled in relation to gross, net lettable or workspace areas. Location-related costs are usually consumables used at various points throughout the building.

In order to understand this concept better, think about heat, light, power, compressed air consumed intensely in particular locations around a major manufacturing plant. These locations may be ideal for use as cost centres as part of a devolved management responsibility. Simpler everyday examples in an office environment would include coffee and tea vending points, photocopying, stationery and computer floppy disks.

Take photocopying as an example; imagine several copiers scattered around an office block with free access by staff. Everybody when presented with easy access to a copier makes free use of the service. Many copies made are a perceived necessity or convenience that in truth are only a waste of money and paper. Then there are the private copies sneaked in with legitimate copying; soon it is a hundred copies for this club and another hundred as a favour to a friend. The problem is that the business is paying and the overhead is being inflated, and that jeopardises jobs.

The facilities manager now has an easy system for monitoring these costs. Using the CAD system to identify, in our example, photocopying stations on the plans each with a unique reference, a database is generated into which is logged the copying costs for each machine, together with the meter readings of the number and type of copies made.

The first check is that the agreed service unit cost is being used to raise the supplier's invoices. The second check compares the throughput of copies, over all similar machines in the building. The idea here is to avoid excessively high load on some machines and also under-utilisation of others.

These are simple overview checks, but where high copying volumes are generated that become a significant overhead cost, more sophisticated checks become necessary.

The logging by individuals of copies taken against job numbers or personal codes becomes a record to add to the database that helps to identify problem locations suitable for more detailed investigation. A few seemingly random checks that discover excesses soon become known and usually are all that is necessary for individuals to think economically. Devolved management works well here in large organisations, with the facilities manager using his overview of the entire organisation to alert section managers to local problems.

3.3   Proportional costs

The allocation of costs of common areas not directly used by anyone or anything in the business would normally be done by spreading them proportionally over the working parts of the building that they service. This will have been done already in the workspace cost calculation, but in certain buildings of mixed use, like a factory with administrative offices, the true workspace cost should be calculated on each class of use. A more accurate measure of the workspace cost is achieved in this way, as the cost of indirect spaces servicing, for example, only the offices, does not get allocated over the factory element, so avoiding penalising factory workspace costs and makes the office space carry its true overhead.

Proportional cost occurs in another context in mixed use buildings where the total efficiency of the business is affected by the mix of areas allocated to each class of use. The mix will have been established from an operational ideal through the space planning exercise, but again the analysis of cost of each class with its directly attached common costs included is a financial review of the mix established on the space criteria.

The questions to be asked are:

- Is the workspace cost for each class competitive?
- Is the overall workspace cost competitive?

Can the overall workspace cost be improved by adjusting the mix of high and low cost classes?

3.4   Cheapest solution v. best space

This is the epitome of the dispute between the financial director and the production director.

The director holding the purse strings will always tend to look at buildings in strict terms of cost, even more so once you, as the facilities manager, have alerted him to just how much it costs to provide workspace. Business at top management level carries a heavy influence of cost and accounting, after all the balance sheet and cashflow are the life blood. The production director has a much more difficult case to argue; he cannot support his case on figures alone but needs to convince the accountants in the finance department that lowest spend does not automatically mean higher profits. The facilities manager is the neutral party standing between the opposing points of view. The graph in Figure 3.3 shows the interaction between these conflicting factors; the choice will finally be determined by setting the priorities of the factors.

Imagine you are that facilities manager, you are collecting and analysing cost data in budget forecasts, actual expenditure and variance reports on the business's premises. This can amount to almost half the total assets of the business but your judgement is needed to achieve value for money.

How does value for money differ from the cheapest cost? Take as an example the case where you are asked to accommodate a sales department relocated from the city centre headquarters to your out-of-town administrative centre. The reasons for the relocation are all sound: good road access, parking and the space in the city centre is expensive and can be easily sublet. The problem is that you are an efficient manager and do not have spare capacity at the out-of-town location to accommodate the twenty-five members of the sales team. The finance director is looking to you for instant action. After all the board has made the

INTERACTION OF WORKSPACE COSTS AND VALUE FOR MONEY

The statistics in the following table show the cost of space in units of 100 sq metres, in column 4 as a multiple of workspace cost and in column 6 adjusted by productivity factors to represent value for money.

1 space units sq m/00	2 rent £/sq m	3 workspace rent/cost factor	4 workspace cost £/000	5 productivity factor %	6 value for money £/000
1	130	×7	91	100	91
2	130	×7	182	105	173
3	130	×6	234	105	223
4	130	×6	312	107	292
5	130	×5	325	110	295
6	130	×5	390	115	339
7	130	×4	364	122	298
8	130	×4	416	112	371
9	130	×3	351	103	341
10	130	×3	390	94	415

The statistics in columns 4 and 6 plot graphically as follows:

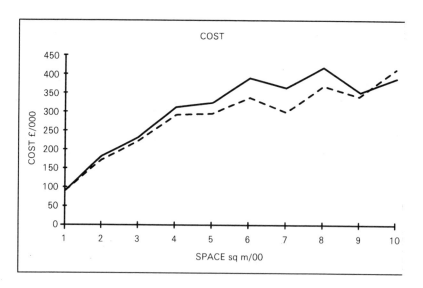

Figure 3.3   *Interaction of workspace costs and value for money*

decision to relocate and a sub-tenant is lined up for the vacated space. The out-of-town location has plenty of site space, so why not buy a few prefabricated buildings and set them out in the car park. Planning restrictions are not a problem and that will solve the matter quickly and cheaply.

As you can guess the sales director is not too keen to move out of a proper office into a building that he believes to have the credibility of a mobile home.

Now set out a management plan:

- Quantify the accommodation required.
- Establish the latest date for the completed relocation.
- Enlist the sales director's support in agreeing at board level the importance of the sales department. The sales team is probably the major source of new business.

Set out the accommodation options:

- Prefabricated solution.
- Build an extension.
- Rent other available space.
- Cost the options.
- Present the options to the board for a decision.

Given a logical approach, common sense will prevail and even if the sales department has to move quickly there will be a temporary solution with a permanent conclusion to follow.

That was a hypothetical situation but one that mirrors the insular approach to business policy decisions. It is not deliberate, but senior management often do not have the supporting information to make fully balanced judgements. The increasing awareness of facilities management is being reinforced by the need for greater national and international competitiveness and by the ability of CAFM systems in particular to provide data analysis that is current.

So who wins the dispute between cheapest and best? The business of course.

4   Maintenance and Feedback

4.1   Routine preventive maintenance

Much has been written in the past about the virtues of preventive maintenance, but to be truly effective the system needs to collect and interpret performance data. We are concerned here with all aspects of the property fabric, including external works, infrastructure and equipment. Even the most robust structure will fall into decay if neglected long enough; the aim here is to establish the compromise between repair, replacement and servicing (usually cost factors in management's perception) and useful function.

Pressure will always be exerted to keep down costs, sometimes at the expense of reliability, and as a result often demonstrated by FM systems to be of no real saving at all.

Routine preventive maintenance requires a plan prepared at the outset by a combination of experience gained on similar facilities, imagination, life cycle data and the operator's priorities. It is easy to create a log of all the components in a maintenance plan; nearly all factory produced components have life expectancy data available, but this is not enough to create the plan. The use of the component within a typical 24-hour or greater time span must be assessed in order to convert the life in running hours into a calendar period.

When reviewing this stage with a building user most lay clients understand the car analogy of services once a year or every 10 000 miles. That is planned preventive maintenance, but it does not work with buildings. The fundamental difference is that each component in the building does not have an owner or driver with a service book and the responsibility to ensure compliance with the attention milestones.

We are faced, as the experts, with creating a self-prompting system for a vast variety of items. On a CAFM system the log of components already mentioned is created on the record drawings with the interface preparing a database. The drawing in Figure 4.1 illustrates the point where the RPM codes are maintenance-based and used to access the relevant section of the database. The drawing reference is limited to specific identification of the component and its location within the

32

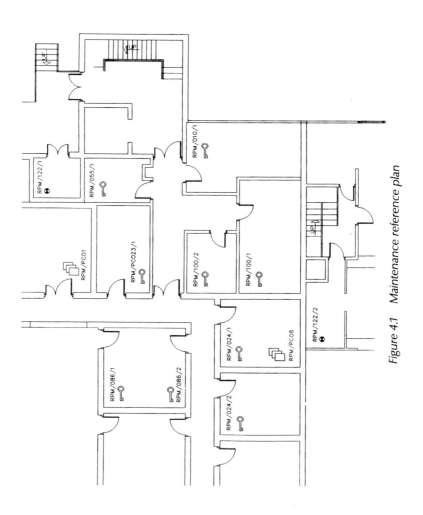

Figure 4.1   Maintenance reference plan

MAINTENANCE DATABASE : LOCK SERVICING REPORT								datapoint Dec-93	
location		code	last	freq	next	zone	cost	breakdown	
	action		date	(wks)	date	code	£	event	cat
	locks	RPM							
G06		023/1	20-May-93	26	18-Nov-93	AZ01	3.26		
G07		024/1	20-May-93	52	20-May-94	AZ01	3.26		
G08	inspect, lubricate,	024/2	20-May-93	52	20-May-94	AZ01	3.26		
G13	adjust and verify	086/1	20-May-93	26	18-Nov-93	PZ01	3.26	08-Aug-93	3.06
G13	key zoning	086/2	20-May-93	26	18-Nov-93	PZ02	3.26		
G17		010/1	20-May-93	52	20-May-94	EZ01	3.26		
G18		100/1	20-May-93	26	18-Nov-93	SZ01	3.26		
G19		100/2	20-May-93	26	18-Nov-93	SZ01	3.26		
G20		055/1	20-May-93	52	25-May-94	SZ03	3.26	08-Sep-93	3.01
G20								18-Nov-93	4.01

Figure 4.2   Maintenance database: lock servicing report

building. The database extract in Figure 4.2 shows this data entered in the first two fields of Location and Action. Once set up, the remaining data is collated within the database adding as many additional fields (columns) as required. In the case of a maintenance plan the date of the last inspection is the springing off point. The next, and probably the most difficult, judgement is deciding on the frequency of inspections or services and here a number of factors have to be considered:

- Expected operational life (running hours).
- Use cycle assessment.
- Strategic importance.
- Access restrictions.
- Back-up systems.
- Cost.

The combination of the first two factors above establishes the calendar life of the component and places a latest milestone on routine action. This milestone is adjusted progressively by the remaining factors, simple components can become key items that must not fail in service. Consider as an example floodlight bulbs, used to highlight an imposing facade; it is no more than an irritation for one to fail and await replacement the next day. The same lamp used to illuminate a high security establishment becomes a different matter. In this and many other examples the experienced judgement of the facilities manager is essential to establish with the user the significance of components and to set a higher incidence of planned action than that indicated by the first calendar milestone.

Access restrictions to parts of the premises can frustrate the best planned schedules, so the use of the premises and any restrictions to free access for maintenance again must be reviewed with the user. This will vary the initial calendar milestones. The frequency so established is entered into the database which then, in conjunction with the 'last date', calculates the next service or inspection date. Essential systems rendered inaccessible by the use of the premises should have been identified in the original construction brief and back-up arrangements made. It is sometimes overlooked especially where the building is not a bespoke design but an adaptation. A recommendation to modify or provide back-up components is not often popular with clients if the investment is heavy, but a carefully researched maintenance plan is useful in highlighting the risks.

It is a fact that many commercial organisations budget very carefully but tend to control costs in compartments dictated by their operation, and then fail to consolidate the facilities costs. An example of this concerned a large manufacturing plant with a chain of processes arranged on the site to allow a controlled flow of production. Sections of the plant and equipment were expensive in capital investment terms, and also to maintain when idle. Each process had a manager with an operating budget that included maintenance. The temptation of the line managers in the early stages of input, raw material handling was to push maintenance to the limits of time, risking breakdown, but showing savings on his operating budget. The knock-on effect on the later processes with high safety requirements and idle time costs far outweighed the earlier benefits. The introduction of a planned maintenance system, controlled by the general manager, removed maintenance from the line manager's budgets, allowing it to react to both strategic and access considerations. The rest is history: output became more consistent, manpower was reduced, overhead recovery benefited and the overall maintenance budget did not increase.

4.2 Emergency cover

The prime function of routine preventive maintenance is to avoid, or at least effectively reduce, the risk of emergency breakdown. No matter how detailed the research no system can be expected to be foolproof, so breakdowns will occur. The causes are many, the most common are:

- Component failure within projected life span.
- Vandalism.
- Maintenance failure.
- Human error.
- Damage.

With any component, and in spite of the best quality monitoring in manufacture, a certain percentage will suffer premature failure. Great strides have been made in recent years through systems like total quality management (TQM) and the Japanese approach towards eradicating manufacturing faults, which have reduced such events dramatically. Premature failure will remain with us and, even if the odds are bettered tenfold, emergencies will still occur as a result.

Facilities managers have a professional responsibility to recognise the existence of premature failure and protect their employers or clients from the less pleasant effects of failure. The fundamental approach to this is already described: that of applying factors to adjust the active life span of a component in line with its level of use, strategic importance, access restrictions and the like. A properly formulated routine preventive maintenance programme, combined with ever-improving component build quality, should remove the risk of shut-down through premature component failure. The sample database shown in Figure 4.2 contains all the necessary information to run a maintenance routine. It identifies the component, describes the activities required, logs the last action date, and using the predetermined frequency periods, calculates the next action date. The cost columns added to the right control expenditure and monitor the budgets.

The remaining four causes are different, as they all contain external factors over which the facilities manager has no control.

Vandalism needs no explanation here and, as far as effect is concerned, physical damage through accident or weather is the same problem. They are not lifespan-related, usually totally random and always highly inconvenient.

The factors of maintenance failure and human error are different, as both are shortcomings of management or systems. Maintenance is at the mercy of human error and can let down the best arranged programme by the failings of carelessness, forgetfulness or, worst of all, laziness.

The facilities manager strives to eliminate these human problems by monitoring operatives' or contractor's performance, arranging supervising and quality spot checking. The personal acceptability of individuals for the quality of their work is a major debate, probably best left to experts in personnel and employment law, but remember the airline approach to flying: each aircraft has two pilots who conduct a set routine of checking and cross-checking each other before take off. Once airborne they are totally committed and the risks are no less with many buildings or plant under the responsibility of a facilities manager.

While the aim is to eliminate emergency stoppages, they will occur, and systems are needed to deal with them with a level of urgency commensurate with the problem.

The exercise of establishing the identity of strategic components is the basis here of creating the emergency routines. These routines need to define clearly:

- Skills to be activated.
- Response time.
- Contact routes.
- Responsibility trails.

When devising routines imagine the most inconvenient time for the emergency, perhaps midnight on Christmas Eve, and write the procedures accordingly. Remember also that it may fall to relatively junior and inexperienced staff to handle the initial actions, so clear step-by-step instructions matter.

The skills and trades to be mobilised should be set down in detail for each anticipated breakdown with clearly defined contact routes by name and telephone/telex/fax. Response times are dictated by the urgency of the repair and can range from one to twenty-four hours. The maintenance database will generate work dockets like the example in Figure 4.3 containing all the necessary contact information.

The responsibility trail is important, once the emergency call out is activated, as at predetermined stages higher managers will need to be informed. Each routine is designed to suit and as an example Figure 4.4 shows a graphical routine procedure.

On complex facilities a CAFM system is the ideal platform to prompt the procedures and drive the duty manager, while under stress, through the system.

WORK DOCKET

Contract ref: _____

Contractor: _____

Date: _____

Maintenance code: RPM

Activity: Locks - inspect, lubricate, adjust and verify key zoning (where applicable)

LOCATION	CODE	INSPECT	LUBE	ADJUST	ZONING	ALL OK
G06	RPM023/1	☐	☐	☐	☐	☐
G07	RPM024/1	☐	☐	☐	☐	☐
G08	RPM024/2	☐	☐	☐	☐	☐
G13	RPM086/1	☐	☐	☐	☐	☐
G13	RPM086/1	☐	☐	☐	☐	☐
G17	RPM010/1	☐	☐	☐	☐	☐
G18	RPM100/1	☐	☐	☐	☐	☐
G19	RPM100/2	☐	☐	☐	☐	☐
G20	RPM055/1	☐	☐		☐	☐

Additional work done: _____

Operative's name _____   time/hrs   rate £/hr   cost £

Materials _____   price

Faults found _____

TOTAL COST   £ [____]

Operative's signature _____

Supervisor's signature _____

Figure 4.3   Work docket

RESPONSIBILITY TRAIL   Date: *10/11/93*

Breakdown description: *Pump failure on primary circulation - Block B space heating -*
                          standby pump available max 7 days

Location code: *BLK B/GF10*
Contractor: *Pump Services Ltd*
Contractor contact: *John Williams*
Tel: *743271*   Fax: *745207*
Response cat: *IM/01 (urgent)*   Time: *3hrs*

Programme

Activities	Period hrs	Target complete	Achieved complete	Variance hrs	Overrun flag
FACILITIES MANAGER					
log breakdown	3	10-Nov-93	10/11/93 10.00		/
contractor call-out	3	10-Nov-93	10-Nov-93		/
accept repair	12	15/11/93 12.00	15/11/93 16.00	-4	non critical
CONTRACTOR					
respond/mobilise	24	11/11/93 14.00	12/11/93 08.00	-18	critical
repair action	72	14/11/93 14.00	14/11/93 22.00	-8	critical
re-commission	8	14/11/93 22.00	15/11/93 08.00	-10	critical
handover	2	14/11/93 24.00	15/11/93 10.00	-10	non critical

Figure 4.4   Responsibility trail

4.3   Control of maintenance personnel

Where a user employs maintenance personnel in-house, the management function of allocating these resources, ensuring efficient service
and monitoring quality, becomes the responsibility of the facilities manager.

The resource available is finite with the in-house approach and while
non-essential maintenance can be scheduled on a first-come first-
served basis, the system needs to be responsive to emergency and
priority calls upon the skills. The 'he who shouts loudest' approach has
no place in this strategy and the facilities manager must be familiar with
the premises and able to make sensible reasoned judgements.

Care is needed in the direction of in-house personnel whenever
components or equipment within the facility are covered by external
service agreements. The demarcation needs to be clear to avoid
unauthorised attention to breakdowns that could invalidate warranties.

There are advantages and disadvantages in having a maintenance department; the main advantages being continuity of staff with benefits in security terms. The disadvantages when compared with engaging a term contractor are lack of flexibility and management involvement.

A worthwhile compromise is to provide janitorial services in-house, covering day-to-day items like replacing light bulbs, refuse disposal, towel replacement and minor odd-jobbing. The more skilled requirements of maintenance can then be provided by external contractors.

For smaller or less complex buildings there are many contractors offering maintenance services on a casual call-out basis covering the disciplines of building and M&E services.

Larger and more complex establishments and those with essential services need a higher degree of response. In such cases the solution is to engage term contractors with the skills and resources available to meet the need. The contractor then becomes responsible for supplying adequate staff skills and resources, materials and spares, together with supervision to ensure quality.

The selection and appointment of term contractors is a skilled process with care needed to write the initial enquiry inviting tenders. The enquiry is the specification of the services to be contractually offered and must cover:

- Term of the contract (1 year, 2 years, etc.).
- Response times.
- Register of components relevant to each contract.
- Security requirements.
- Employer's restrictions (limited working hours, etc.).
- Time and cost recording documentation.
- Schedule of rates for contractor to price.
- Out-of-hours call-out charges.

This list is indicative and will be expanded as necessary for each contract to cover all anticipated events. The better the enquiry is drafted, the less the risk of claims and extraordinary charges.

With this approach competitive tenders can be invited from more than one contractor, this providing a self-regulating basis for achieving the best current market price for these services.

Having now created the routine preventive maintenance plan and secured the personnel to carry it out, the facilities manager needs to co-ordinate the plan's implementation.

Reference back to Figure 4.2 shows a typical maintenance database print-out with dates of last activity and next activity clearly shown.

The beauty of using databases for this exercise is the ease of interrogation and generation of extract reports. When running a routine maintenance programme the database is asked to reconfigure in ascending date order of the Next Date Field, after which the activities programmed for a specific future period are obvious.

Figure 4.5 shows an extract from the database listing the activities scheduled for a seven-day period.

The immediate future activity listing is printed out as an extract report and used to generate work dockets instructing the maintenance staff. The work docket (see the sample in Figure 4.3) also serves as a quality prompt by listing out the steps in each activity and requiring the operative to acknowledge completion. There is space to note relevant comments on additional work needed and, with this information, costs are monitored and invoices checked. The completed docket returns to the facilities manager and is used to update the maintenance database.

This approach adds a further quality check in that arranging the database in progressive date order highlights any activities that are late.

MAINTENANCE DATABASE : 7 DAY ACTIVITY LISTING
WEEK BEGINNING : 15/11/93

location	action	code	action date	completed
	extract fans	**RPM**		
G27	check flow, check delay & clean filter	122/1	15-Nov-93	Y
G28	check flow, check delay & clean filter	122/2	15-Nov-93	Y
	window cleaning			
BLC	external Block C	303/1	16-Nov-93	
BLB	internal Block B	302/1	16-Nov-93	Y
	printers			
F132	strip, clean, service & adjust UTAX	PC01	17-Nov-93	Y
G07	service, adjust & test Canon NP6650	PC08	17-Nov-93	
	locks			
G06	inspect, lubricate, adjust & verify key zoning	023/1	18-Nov-93	
G13		086/1	18-Nov-93	
G13		086/2	18-Nov-93	
G18		100/1	18-Nov-93	
G19		100/2	18-Nov-93	

Figure 4.5   Maintenance database: 7-day activity listing

4.4   Cost control

Budgeting is all-important to successful facilities management, not just the setting of quarterly or annual budgets, but monitoring expenditure against the budget.

The maintenance database extends beyond the calendar fields into one of cost, this being established from, in the case of external term contractors, the tendered rates. Using the reconfigure function in the database to arrange in date order creates a cashflow that can easily show quarterly, monthly or even weekly budget limits.

Once actual costs incurred have been entered from the costed work dockets, into the next field on the database, they can be compared with the calendar-related budgets to generate variance reports that highlight over and underspending.

Sensible financial management understands that budgets are always a prediction with the main purpose of providing a model on which to monitor actual costs. It is prudent, therefore, whenever a variance occurs to take the cost adjustment into a contingency calculation. Thus underspending increases the contingency whereas overspend reduces it. The goal is to keep the contingency column in overall credit.

The budget costs, shown together with the actual costs recorded and calculated variances, may constitute annual statistics to conform with the company's accounting conventions, but maintenance cannot be contained by annuality, it is ongoing. The contingency column continues therefore on a rolling basis, being adjusted back to zero as each new annual budget is struck by either subtracting any accrued surplus from the new budget, or adding deficits.

4.5   Health and safety

The legal requirements for inspection and safety certification of safety equipment, electrical apparatus, general building fabric and equipment is steadily growing with dramatically increased personal liability for company directors and facilities managers.

The regular inspection and maintenance of fire fighting equipment, and the testing of alarms and smoke detection is very appropriate for CAFM control. What better than logging all fire extinguishers, hose reels, alarm buttons and the like on computer-generated layout plans. Checking becomes easily monitored, the risk of missing an item check is removed, and missing or misplaced portable equipment like fire extinguishers is discovered. The usual database interface generates the summary information and work dockets as before and the safety file gains proper records of discharge of statutory obligations that will satisfy the inspectors.

The same principle applies to electrical equipment, lifts, escalators and air-conditioning systems.

4.6   Feedback

Informed decisions are created by a combination of past experience and historical data, and better judgement depends on feedback of information. Every time an unscheduled event occurs it should be logged to the maintenance database and a field for this purpose set up. There are many categories of breakdown or performance shortcomings; some are specific to each installation but the following list is universal:

- Maintenance operative's performance (1.0).
- Term contractor's performance (2.0).
- Component failure within life expectancy (3.0).
- Inadequate maintenance procedures (4.0).

If each activity is coded with a reference, e.g. maintenance operative's performance is 1.0, term contractor's performance is 2.0, etc., this code is inserted in the database field as shown in Figure 4.2. Whenever a review of breakdowns is needed, the database is reconfigured on the field as shown also in Figure 4.6. Now it becomes obvious that components are failing too often within their expected lifespan. This is statistical feedback.

MAINTENANCE DATABASE : BREAKDOWN EXTRACT REPORT							datapoint Dec-93	
location		code	last	freq	next	zone	cost	breakdown
	action		date	(wks)	date	code	£	event	cat
	locks	RPM							
G20	inspect, lubricate,	055/1	20-May-93	52	25-May-94	SZ03	3.26	08-Sep-93	3.01
G20	adjust and verify							18-Nov-93	4.01
G13	key zoning	086/1	20-May-93	26	18-Nov-93	PZ01	3.26	08-Aug-93	3.06

Figure 4.6   Maintenance database: breakdown extract report

Technical feedback requires further investigation to discover any common causes of breakdown. Is the component being abused, over-loaded or under-maintained? Is there a quality deficiency in the component?

Corrective action becomes focused; for example, replace component with heavier duty item, shorten maintenance intervals.

A quality deficiency raises other considerations; for example, the pump failure highlighted on the database extract. How many other pumps of this model are in use throughout the building, how strategic are they to the operation and how can other unscheduled breakdowns be avoided? Now comes reactive preventive maintenance, where each corresponding pump is removed from service on a planned programme, stripped, tested and not returned to service until quality checked. Obviously, the planned programme prioritises the order of decommissioning/recommissioning to attend to those pumps at greatest risk and with the greatest knock-on effect.

If a pattern of breakdown becomes repetitive then the corrective action is inadequate and must be reviewed.

The long-term benefit of feedback is to improve quality in future component design together with influencing future design briefs for new buildings. Any architect or designer operating a quality assurance system depends on feedback for improvement and is required under ISO 9000 in design output to identify the characteristics for safe and proper function.

5 Operational Services

Up to this point we have covered the activities of how an organisation fits into a building through the space planning and costing exercises. We have also considered the maintenance of the building fabric and its service installations. We have not considered those services within the facilities manager's remit that support the core tasks of the business.

Having provided and taken steps to perpetuate the working environment, it becomes essential that the business can operate efficiently within the environment. The provision of operational services secures that position.

We are not servicing the building, but we are servicing the occupants and equipment that make up the business. A typical range of operational sources includes:

- Security.
- Catering and staff welfare.
- Creche provisions.
- Cleaning/waste disposal.
- Internal communications.
- Energy distribution.
- Partnering arrangements.

The facilities manager will need to research the appropriate list of services for each location and keep it under review to improve the support and react to changing conditions. This typical list will serve as a prompt for the next sections of this chapter but in real-life situations you will need to be imaginative and innovative.

5.1 Security

The range here is wide, starting from basic reception duties through to the full-scale, high security requirements.

The provision of a receptionist is the province of personnel management, but how that reception controls and monitors access in and out of a building depends for its effectiveness on several facilities management considerations.

45

The first is location within the building, the next is means of communication. These are obvious, but think further; will there be a relief receptionist to allow continuous cover during all working hours? If not, should the public entrance area and reception be secure, preventing casual or opportunist entry further into the building? In city centre locations, much casual theft occurs through breaches in reception security. There are many physical security systems available to restrict casual access; digital locks, card entry systems, security screens, closed-circuit television. As stated earlier, you need to be imaginative and innovative.

If using a physical control system, remember to include the lifts at all entry points available to the public. These systems, together with more basic key suiting, are valuable in regulating staff access where certain high security areas, because of confidentiality or processes, require restricted access.

Lifts are a particular source of problems, as often it is not enough simply to control access at the ground floor. Basement car parks are high-risk areas for unauthorised entry and, once into the lift, it becomes easy to bypass the reception. Basement car parks have other problems, not least of which are staff safety and vehicle theft. Many such car parks are controlled during working hours by simple vehicle barriers that are effective enough in preventing illicit parking, but not intruder-proof. The natural reaction is to install security shutters, but how will they be operated? Vehicle sensing is too easily breached to be effective; card operation will cause unacceptable delays at peak times and again will not defeat the ingenuity of an intruder. CCTV surveillance is a deterrent, but is only really effective if constantly monitored.

There is no conclusive answer to this common problem. The building security can be made intruder-proof by preventing access directly from the car park that bypasses the public reception. CCTV will give some confidence to staff on their personal safety and that of their cars, but there is no another factor. Terrorist attacks appear to be totally random and devastating in their disruption of business. The top of the security scale is required by many government establishments and by certain commercial organisations. The need for high security is usually to maintain confidentiality of information, either strategic or commercial, and also to prevent interference.

When devising security systems to prevent external challenges from succeeding, try to anticipate how these would be staged. There is forced intrusion on the one hand, and intrusion by stealth on the other. If force is anticipated, where the attack is intended to disrupt or for petty theft, for example ram raiding, then vehicle obstacles will be a deterrent. Carefully planned access routes with soft landscaping, well placed bollards, sufficient structural integrity in vulnerable parts of the building and even water features, moats and the like will discourage effectively. Intrusion by stealth is more difficult, as it depends on the human factor. Almost all stealth breaches in a properly devised security system are the result of human failings.

Here we are approaching the province of quality management which strives to eliminate the human factor. This will never be achieved, but the facilities manager and the designer of the building in co-operation can provide the physical systems that give the quality manager the means to progressively reduce the human factor.

The facilities manager can start by devising a checklist of security requirements such as the following:

- Examine the public perimeter of the building or estate and note all possible points of entry.
- Assess the overall security rating of the location and limit points of entry accordingly.
- Identify areas of higher sensitivity and arrange their location to enhance security.
- Anticipate the type of attack.
- Devise physical measures to frustrate the anticipated attack.
- Liaise with the personnel department and quality manager to integrate the human functions with the physical security systems.

This list is not exhaustive but will prompt a dialogue with other managers that develops into a security plan.

The facilities manager needs to monitor the operation of all the physical systems in use and address breakdowns and shortcomings. Any problems caused by human error should be resolved with the personnel department.

5.2   Catering and staff welfare

The degree of staff welfare will be dictated by the size, type and location of the facility. In small organisations it can be restricted to tea and coffee making and perhaps a sandwich delivery service for lunchtime.

The origins of staff welfare can be traced back to the industrialists of the eighteenth and nineteenth centuries who realised that, in spite of the industrial revolution, labour remained a key element in the process. No doubt some of these employers possessed a social conscience, but the hard facts of business economics started staff welfare. Some of the early efforts look squalid now; poor cramped housing, inadequate sanitation but, in comparison with the standard of the day, it was progress indeed. In return for this capital outlay the employer was rewarded with a tied labour force located where he wanted it.

The passage of time has modified these early rigours but the principle remains. If you apply well-judged staff welfare, the reward is higher efficiency and improved productivity.

So, when devising welfare arrangements, bear in mind that it will be an overhead burden on the business that needs to be justified by returns realised in the product. Building a reputation of looking after staff engenders loyalty and attracts quality individuals to work for the business, particularly in buoyant times when competition is strong.

There are key factors to analyse in setting the level of welfare.

- Size of labour force.
- Mix of labour force by job type, sex, type of employment, e.g. full- or part-time.
- Location of workplace.
- Unusual working hours.
- Competitor's attitude.

Clearly there is a minimum staff level that makes it economically viable to provide even subsidised canteen facilities. Whenever it becomes necessary to provide catering the facilities manager is faced with a choice; does the business engage the catering staff directly and assume the responsibility of produce ordering, together with the ever increasing burden of hygiene regulations? The alternative is to contract out the service to experts who can even control the design and equipping of the kitchens and dining areas. All the facilities manager needs to do to set up the service is select the caterer and provide the space within the building.

Many large organisations with long-established, directly employed catering staff are now contracting out these services.

Whenever contracting out, the specification detailing the precise responsibilities of the specialist needs to be set out along the lines already described in chapter 4 under control of maintenance personnel.

Staff welfare extends beyond eating and drinking, with a choice covering sports facilities from exercise rooms to swimming pools, and sports clubs. All have to be paid for and it is essential that the facilities manager knows exactly how much the provision of accommodation and equipment is costing.

This information, added to directly engaged staff costs or those of contractors must be available and reviewed regularly to verify the cost effectiveness.

Cost effectiveness is a very subjective measurement in terms of employment benefit, but nevertheless the facilities manager charged by the board to provide detailed welfare services must do so on a value-for-money basis. It is useful to measure these costs as a percentage of the overall overhead of the business and monitor changes, especially increases.

On occasions the location, combined with unusual working hours, dictates the need for other welfare provisions. Shopping, hairdressing, medical and dental services on site are fairly common, as are banking, travel and transport. Again it is a matter of analysing each case in depth.

5.3   Creche provisions

There is a great pool of highly trained and motivated labour prevented from working by the lack of child care. The provision of creche facilities is being further encouraged by tax concessions, both corporate and individual, and this can be the way back to work (even part-time) for valuable members of staff after statutory maternity leave.

It can also provide the edge over competitors in securing the best staff. Welfare provisions that solve immediate personal problems are very cost effective, often making it possible for individuals to work where salary considerations alone are not the prime factor.

The provision of creche facilities can help men as well as women to return to work.

5.4   Cleaning/waste disposal

General cleaning and janitorial services are a routine maintenance item and have been dealt with in chapter 4. There are, however, occasions when specialist cleaning and decontamination is required. This becomes an operational service, as it is a direct requirement of the business processes.

Experience of a cross-section of industrial, commercial and other building users has thrown up a great variety of cleaning and waste disposal requirements both of a routine and, on occasions, emergency nature.

The routine requirements are straightforward, being dictated on a regular basis by the business process and the intensity of working.

The engineering industry, for example, can demand degreasing services either as an in-house service or bought in from a sub-contractor. Routine maintenance and process plant where general contamination can enter and disrupt the reinstated process must be thoroughly flushed or otherwise removed before recommissioning.

Imagine the consequences in the food industry; indeed on the odd occasions when contamination does occur, the ramifications of removing all of a given manufacturing batch, often even from the supermarket shelves, are costly in real terms and immeasurable in damage to customer confidence.

Emergency cleaning most commonly results from spillage of either toxic chemicals or other substances that render the process unsafe to operate. Whenever substances requiring specialist control and neutralisation procedures are present then Health and Safety legislation requires the proper attention to emergency action. It is, however, too late to react to specialist training once an incident occurs; the necessary personnel and equipment must already be available. This could be your responsibility as the plant facilities manager.

Our ever-increasing concern about the environment and public safety is making waste disposal an increasing financial burden on industry. The safe disposal of physically dangerous material like engineering swarf and carcinogenic waste such as used engine oil can no longer be by general dumping and, as many of these waste items have realisable scrap value, it is always worth investigating selective waste storage and disposal.

It is tempting for general waste disposal, particularly in liquid form, to be into the foul drainage system. This must strictly comply with all current legislation governing outfall quality, so a sampling system is needed to maintain standards. Again this is a service that often lands on the facilities manager's desk, not because he is an expert in microbiology, but because he is expert in setting up support services and monitoring their function.

Disposal methods are important – the simple matters of type of waste containers, who will empty them and how often and where they will be sited to suit the process, but still be accessible sometimes out of hours for disposal.

The value of scrap waste has been mentioned, with selection and sorting to separate waste with recoverable value from that for general disposal. Most offices can already benefit from separating recyclable paper waste from used coffee cups and sandwich wrappers. If the volume is great enough there are paper recovery firms that will pay by weight to take it away. Lesser volumes will usually be removed free of charge; there is no cash benefit, but it saves trees.

5.5   Internal communications

Communication is the essential quality of good management; even sole traders cannot succeed without communicating. We are more concerned here with organisations that rely on many individuals striving in unison towards the common goal that is the success of the business. In order to accomplish this they must be able to communicate with each other easily. The facilities manager does not define chains of command or arrange the management; that is for the board of directors to decide and delegate downwards. Once the lines of communication are defined a system is necessary to allow easy spoken contact, written contact and electronic contact.

So we have space planning in here at the beginning, grouping individuals in the building to simplify face-to-face contact; next we have remote spoken contact through internal and external telephones and paging systems.

Written communication is by mail, including internal memoranda, and electronic communication covers facsimile, telex and workstation networking.

The operation of all these systems is the job of the facilities manager. Simple services often cause maximum aggravation if not controlled. As an example, take the internal telephone system of a large organisation where the nature of the business dictates a significant and regular churn in the occupation. Traditionally, the internal telephone directory is published as a printed booklet and from time to time amendments are issued to bring it up to date with staff changes.

It is more often than not out of date and it relies on every member of staff being methodical in logging the changes as they are notified. Soon the internal directory is a confusing mess.

Using the CAFM system all the internal and external telephone points are logged to a plan of the building showing their extension numbers. We have the start of a communications database. As existing staff are moved around the building they are moved electronically on the CAFM system by picking them up on screen and moving them to the new location. The revised extension numbers are activated on the system and the vacated extensions are marked as free. The database is updated from the drawing revisions and published as the telephone directory. The examples in Figures 5.1 and 5.2 show samples of a CAFM plan and the internal directory generated from it.

Using this system means that never again will the internal directories rely on individuals to update them and they will always be current.

New staff coming into the building will be placed on the plan and the free extension numbers for that workstation allotted to them in the directory.

There is a further service available on this system and that is to log the location of individual staff within the organisation. This can be very useful on complex estates and a valuable time-saving aid to show staff wishing to find a particular contact. Reference to a computer terminal linked to the CAFM system will allow an enquiry to be made by interrogating the directory database, then tracing the location on the estate plans by either the building/room reference or even the extension numbers. If the enquirer is unfamiliar with the estate layout a location extract of the plan can be printed out on a laser printer and used as a map.

As these staff records are now a database, additional fields can be added at will without the information in them appearing on the CAFM plans. This data can even be confidential staff records logged here to assist the personnel department in their administration of the workforce. Confidentiality is maintained by password control of the full database that restricts general browsing to non-sensitive details.

Just as telephone extensions are logged to the CAFM system, so can facsimile machines, telex machines and also terminal modems and networks be added. With this information the communications systems are arranged to link according to the lines dictated by the senior management and security blocks are properly positioned to prevent access to sensitive information.

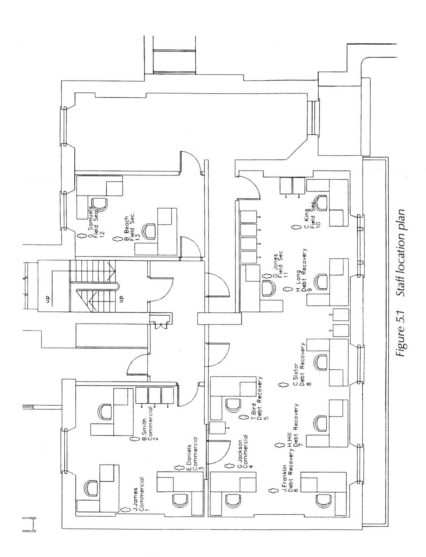

Figure 5.1   Staff location plan

INTERNAL TELEPHONE DIRECTORY

Page no :	1			Issue date :		01-Nov-93
EMPLOYEE	**JOB**	**EXTENSION**	**INTERCOM**	**WP**	**WP REF**	
Beach B	field sec	213	105	13	09/111	
Bird T	debt recovery	205	101	5	122/09	
Daniels E	commercial	203	100	3	11/9878	
Franklin J	debt recovery	206	102	6	12/098	
Hill H	debt recovery	207	103	7	10/001	
Jackson G	commercial	204	101	4	12/006	
James J	commercial	200	100	1	12/006	
Jones G	field sec	211	104	11	16/032	
King C	field sec	210	104	10	10/003	
Long H	debt recovery	209	104	- 9	19/432	
Samuels G	field sec	212	105	12	02/200	
Slater C	debt recovery	208	103	8	19/321	
Smith B	commercial	201	100	2	100/233	

Figure 5.2   Internal telephone directory

Clearly shown networking diagrams on CAFM are invaluable in the unfortunate event of a computer virus becoming active in the system. The speed of response of the CAFM system allows damage limitation measures to be effective by effectively isolating the virus.

5.6   Energy distribution

Energy and services that provide point-of-use supply from a central distribution point can be complex and once installed inflexible. This distribution obviously includes power but it also covers process gases, compressed air, steam, lubricants and the like. It is useful to log the supply points of each service throughout the building together with the service routes from the central supply. Hospital buildings benefit from this CAFM data, with their multitude of gas, air and vacuum service points.

Vehicle servicing installations have compressed air, steam cleaning and lubricants on distribution systems. All have to be monitored, serviced and checked regularly against their performance tolerances.

The monitoring and checking is driven by a CAFM-generated database along the lines of the planned maintenance system shown in chapter 4.

The management principle here is again to log all the location data and basic specifications to a CAFM plan and use this to generate a series of databases, one to each service, showing location, reference and performance specification. A calendar of actions covering servicing and monitoring is added and that generates dockets requiring information feedback on the system condition and performance.

5.7 Partnering

This is a term well understood across the Atlantic and it describes a unique arrangement of contracting out key support services.

The progression of boom followed by recession is cyclical and will continue into the future; the only unknown is the pitch of the cycle. Given that the stresses of severe recession are strong in current corporate management thinking, one of the results has been a trend away from diversification back to concentration on the core business. The change of emphasis has fuelled the growing awareness of facilities management as an efficiency vehicle and similarly the concentration on core business has called in-house peripheral activities into question. The expertise in manufacturing is in designing, marketing and making a product, not in running a transport network or a warehousing and stockholding service. That is best left to experts in those fields where transport, warehousing and distribution are their core business.

Transport is the classic case and many American companies no longer run their own vehicle fleets.

Weigh up the factors for and against running your own fleet.

In favour:

- Dedicated transport.
- Staff drivers.
- Control over distribution priorities.
- No transport operator taking a profit.
- Vehicles an asset on the balance sheet.

Against:

- Need full-time transport manager.
- Need mechanics and fitters.
- No spare capacity to cover breakdowns.
- Little experience in forming vehicle renewal programmes.
- Inaccurate budgeting.
- Variable costs by taking all the risks.

So why not contract it all out? The concern here is that conventional contracting out is often on a bid basis with the cheapest price winning. This is not a very comfortable way to place the services so essential to the operation of the business. After all, late or unreliable deliveries mean lost customers.

Partnering is different; it involves selecting a specialist partner, a transport company in this case, on the basis of guaranteed and proven service, resources and commitment.

So now you have an operator who can deliver the service with adequate back up. This gives the same level of comfort as dedicated transport and staff drivers generated in the 'in favour' factors of a company running its own fleet.

Control over priorities has been agreed in your discussions on service and, of course, the transport specialist will avoid break down disruption by preventive maintenance, experience and adequate back up.

That leaves the cost factors to settle. You are in a very strong position to negotiate well if you can show a volume of business that makes you your transport partner's major or only source of income. There is nothing wrong with his making a profit; it probably comes to less than the saving that you will make on overheads. You have price certainty as your partner takes the commercial risk on transport costs, so your product costing is more accurate. Lastly, as for the vehicles on the balance sheet, it is much better to reinvest in materials and plant, in fact in anything that directly improves your core business.

Transport is a good example but look at all non-core activities and ask the questions.

Am I an expert in this activity? Is there somebody out there who is an expert and would like my business?

If the answers are no and yes respectively you are a candidate for partnering.

5.8 Benchmarking

Only the most specialised operational activities will be unique to a particular organisation. All other activities will be part of other companies' or organisations' operational methods and by that very factor will be subject to research and development in the quest for improved efficiency, quality and economic return to the organisation. This creates the situation where different organisations invest time and money in parallel research.

The concept of benchmarking has developed through organisations seeking to measure their performance in set activities against that achieved by their competitors. The obvious difficulty here is confidentiality and secrecy between competitors; after all, what company will willingly divulge its performance statistics to help another use the data to catch up with or even overtake it in the market place.

This concept is not generally successful, the only exceptions are the occasional cross-company research and development programmes where the investment exceeds the resources of individual companies. Examples of cross-company cooperation can be seen in the automotive and aerospace industries, for example Volvo, Lancia and Renault have collaborated on a common design for car platforms and more recently Volvo and Mitsubishi have constructed a joint manufacturing plant in Holland. Clearly these collaborations are the exception to the rule and for the most part each manufacturer continues to pursue its own carefully guarded programmes.

The answer for any organisation seeking to benchmark and test its performance statistics is to identify an alternative industry that uses like technology but does not compete directly in the same market place. The barriers to a genuine exchange of data are removed and all parties benefit from joint research.

6 Assets

6.1 Asset registers

Traditionally assets have been logged to inventories that are used as the basis for depreciation calculations, capital allowance assessments and a basic list of the tangible assets of the business. The problem with inventories is that they need considerable effort to create and, unless regularly reviewed, degrade in accuracy through the passage of time. Even computer-generated, database-type inventories are inconvenient.

In order to record an asset properly, certain information is needed to provide a unique identity. The asset must be described unambiguously and its location in the building must be registered. An example will best illustrate this point and the development from basic inventory through to a CAFM asset register.

Let us look at a common item of office equipment, the photocopier, in this case a Canon NP6650. The traditional style inventory for accounting and insurance purposes will show details as in Figure 6.1.

The basic principles are satisfied; the copier is now identified by make and model and the serial number is also noted, so the entry becomes unique. The cost and age of the copier are also entered, so there is the basis of the accounting requirements, but where is it located in the building? If the business has one or two such copiers, then finding a specific one by serial number is simple, but suppose that there are twenty scattered over several office locations and not even in the same town. Adding a location code as in Figure 6.2 positions the item by identifying the geographical location, floor and room.

In chapter 5 on operational services we considered the opportunities to record and analyse usage details by logging copy volumes. The asset register if run as a database can easily import the operational data, thus building up a comprehensive picture of the photocopier's value.

Inventories like this covering all equipment over a pre-determined value become hundreds of pages long in large estates and this is their ultimate weakness. Large inventories are cumbersome to review and update, so the answer is an asset register generated on a computer database from the CAFM plans.

Furniture/equipment inventory (contd.)			
Ground floor room 7			
	swivel chair	2	no
	chair	1	no
	desk	2	no
	filing cabinet	2	no
	typewriters	2	no
	photocopier	1	no
	fire extinguisher	1	no
Ground floor room 8			
	swivel chair	2	no
	chair	1	no
	desk	2	no
	filing cabinet	2	no
	typewriters	2	no
	fire extinguisher	1	no

Figure 6.1   Traditional inventory

As with the maintenance of fixed items logged by CAFM, we can create an asset register using the same principle of marking the copier on the plan in the correct room, attaching a code and using this to start the database by creating the first three columns or fields shown in Figure 6.3. The remaining fields are added at will within the database and loaded with information collated from other sources. The cost and age entries come from the accounts department and operational ser-

61

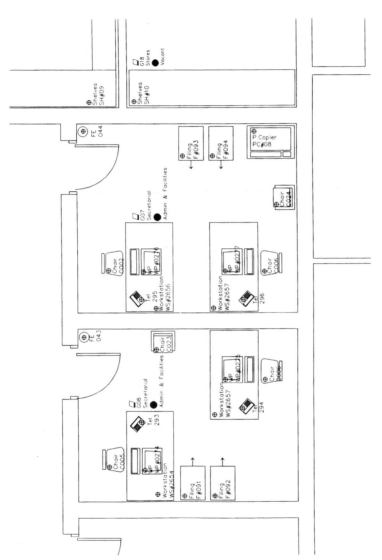

Figure 6.2 Asset location plan

ASSET REGISTER: ROOM INVENTORY EXTRACT REPORT

datapoint Aug-93

room no	occupant	use type	asset	asset ref	value £	age mths	expired life (%)	H&S assessment ref	date
G07	Admin & Facilities	A	swivel chair	C002	56.00	24	35		
			swivel chair	C006	56.00	24	35		
			chair	C024	44.00	24	35		
			workstation	WS2656	326.00	27	45	e26	Feb-93
			workstation	WS2657	326.00	27	45	e27	Feb-93
			filing cabinet	F093	137.00	24	20		
			filing cabinet	F094	137.00	24	20		
			word processor	WP0276	683.00	42	88	e73	Jun-93
			word processor	WP0277	683.00	42	88	e74	Jun-93
			photocopier	PC08	1284.00	28	55	e46	Aug-93
			fire extinguisher	FE044	52.00	12	25	f17	May-93
G08	Admin & Facilities	A	swivel chair	C005	56.00	24	35		
			swivel chair	C006	56.00	24	35		

Figure 6.3   Asset register: room inventory extract report

vices details from the facilities manager's other database on equipment and review prompt dates.

These review dates are again similar to the maintenance database calendar in that different items of equipment in the asset register need to be inspected and checked at intervals. These intervals vary according to use, performance expectation and strategic importance. The next review date is automatically generated in the database using the frequency applied to the previous inspection dates. Work dockets and checklists for the inspections are generated each week/month or at whatever regular interval is deemed appropriate. The database can also be primed to overrule the programmed review dates if usage is particularly high and inspections are triggered by copy count milestones. This is a typical photocopier situation but is equally applicable to other pieces of equipment that require servicing or inspection based on a mix of calendar frequency and use load.

In this way the asset register is active and constantly updated on the principle of a little and often. The main disadvantage of the traditional inventory is avoided and the register becomes a working document in day-to-day management rather than an addendum to the annual accounts and the contents insurance policy.

There is a more obvious direct financial benefit derived from CAFM asset registers than just that of tighter management; annual audits should be simpler, as the business is providing better basic information on assets and there will also be an accurate check on the range of insurance cover needed.

While it is useful to log manufacturer's serial numbers, they are devised primarily for the manufacturer's convenience and are often long and difficult to recognise; the copier example is a case in point. This can be overcome in a database by allocating a reference of your own like that shown in the example. This needs to be clearly and durably displayed on the item of equipment. Electronic tagging and bar coding have the benefit of rapid identification on site with the appropriate readers but are more costly to set up. Alphanumeric codes stencilled on or fixed by high impact labelling are a practical alternative and are easily generated from the database. The label may be restricted to just the item identification code but it is worth considering including a limited amount of key information from the database. Even showing the equipment location reference such as the appropriate room number provides casual confirmation that mobile equipment in particular has been returned to the correct location after use without the need to refer to the asset register.

6.2   Tracking

Assets in the form of tools, equipment and certain furniture are portable, valuable and attractive to individuals. So how do you as the facilities manager protect the company's interests?

The regular register review will discover several irregularities:

- Incomplete equipment.
- Incorrect location.
- Missing altogether.
- Damaged.

The discovery of incomplete equipment most often occurs when the complete unit is a combination of mechanical appliances and consumable accessories. The office first-aid box is an example that is perhaps not very serious, but scale it up to respirators and resuscitation equipment and think of an emergency situation when it is discovered that somebody has stolen the oxygen tubing from the face mask to repair the petrol line in their car. This is where the grading of equipment by strategic importance comes in to increase the frequency of checking to the point where it eliminates equipment failure.

Incorrect location happens all the time; people acquire general equipment and use it as if it is for their personal use; this is not usually serious and is easily corrected at the review. Persistent offenders identify themselves through this system and can be retrained or in severe cases reprimanded.

Before carrying out any such corrective action it is always worth asking why equipment has been moved; on occasions the users have good reason, and their changes are valid. When this happens the answer is to change the CAFM details.

Missing equipment is a problem because when the review system is working properly it is almost impossible for the item to be merely misplaced. It usually has disappeared off site either through theft or accident. In either case security needs to be examined and even the review frequency increased to encourage more care at operator level.

Damage can be accidental, or due to wear and tear or vandalism. In each case tighter review procedures are the answer, with perhaps increased training in the operation of the equipment if the problem is excessive and caused by the first two reasons.

6.3   Equipment performance

The balancing of operational load on equipment was examined in chapter 5 and assuming that this is done it becomes possible to monitor equipment performance and reliability against a controlled datum. Equipment that habitually falls short of measured expectations needs to be reviewed on the basis of overwork, manufacturing quality, servicing quality and better alternatives.

The ability of the facilities manager to collate the data and analyse it into causes will indicate the correct solution.

6.4   Servicing

Whenever equipment requires specialist servicing, either through a service contract or by regular call-out of the specialist, the milestones need to be flagged. With much equipment these milestones depend on both level of usage and timescale. The asset register is an ideal location for this date which can be activated by the operational data.

Apart from the major preventive maintenance value of properly controlled servicing it is usually a precondition in warranty agreements that the equipment is maintained in accordance with the manufacturer's requirements.

There is a potentially dangerous warranty and reliability situation whenever equipment uses consumable stores that are obtained by the business from sources other than the equipment supplier. In the copier example there is great competition to supply copying paper, especially to high volume users. It is important not just to buy the paper on price choice alone but to confirm that it is compatible with the copier and will not cause increased breakdowns or invalidate the warranty. This point should be a positive check item whenever multiple sourcing of equipment and consumables occurs and the list of examples is long; for example, vending machines, fax machines, chemical and salt based water treatment equipment and many more specific to each location.

It is not just the effect on the equipment that must be considered in terms of serviceability, there are safety factors where risk analysis is necessary to ensure operator safety and prevent personal injury.

6.5   Vandalism and damage

The objective is to eliminate premature failure or even partial loss of equipment efficiency as a result of damage. This should not occur as an involuntary act and only acceptable wear and tear is tolerable.

The more innocent forms of damage occur through accident, thoughtlessness and a lack of responsibility in the operators. The first task of the facilities manager in monitoring failures is to categorise them according to cause. Accidental damage or damage caused through carelessness are involuntary events and respond well to training; vandalism is a different problem.

The human aspect of vandalism is the responsibility of security and if the perpetrators are from within the business then it is a matter to be resolved by the personnel department. The facilities manager, however, having identified a problem must examine practical measures that will prevent a recurrence and therefore assist in the management of the personnel.

Equipment located in secluded positions is a temptation and any items containing cash should be sited as visibly as possible. Payphones and vending machines are obvious because the very nature of their service requires prominence, but vending machines in toilets are often sited there to minimise social embarrassment. We have therefore a temptation, a machine containing cash in a secluded location where surveillance is inappropriate so the problem becomes one of managing risk. Deterrents will depend on the level of attempted theft and can range from notices stating that the cash is removed regularly, implying there is never enough to be worth stealing, to physical security in the form of locks and alarms.

Externally-sited cash collecting equipment like parking-ticket machines pose particular problems as vandalism that renders them inoperative can jeopardise the operation of the car park. Here logging to the asset register creates a management system that inspects and ensures satisfactory operation.

6.6 Emergency equipment

This is an emotive section as it implies life and death situations with high levels of urgency. In this context the facilities manager's task is to eliminate the risk of failure whenever any such equipment is activated. Total elimination is impossible, but regular testing and inspection together with back-up arrangements will reduce the risk to acceptable levels. Whenever assessing these risks it is best to start with a risk analysis of the emergency itself; is it people threatening, property threatening or both?

Fire-fighting, alarm and safety equipment is aimed at the first category, with standby generators more probably geared to supportive processes in the event of a mains power failure. Standby power, depending on the process to be supported, can also fall into the overall category of personal and property threat.

There is no all-embracing philosophy in the approach to the facilities management of emergency equipment but as a guide try following an analysis trial. The diagram in Figure 6.4 is a suggested format that can be developed specifically for every location.

The facilities manager needs to be intensely practical whenever the installation and control of emergency equipment is required; he must co-ordinate the expert advice of safety specialists with the limitations imposed by the building.

6.7 People tracking

The tracking of people within a building estate or multi-location organisation is essential to the smooth operation of the organisation. The system for logging people with their workstation equipment to a database using CAFM has already been described under operational services in chapter 5, but it is worth considering here as an extension of asset tracking.

Any business is an amalgam of human and equipment resources in this context, so while the tracking of individual workstations is important to ease communications it is necessary to coordinate staff churn with equipment availability and distribution.

In this case the database of personnel established to satisfy the needs of operational services is interfaced with the asset register. Before the

RISK ANALYSIS   Assmnt date :   23-Nov-93

Item : drinks vending   Ref :   CG34/6

Function: *Vending machine delivering hot beverages on*
demand to staff, no restriction on access or use.
Drinks supplied in individual powder cassettes.

Hazard : *Unguarded boiling water outlet.*

Risk : *Cups are placed under water outlet by hand.*

Safeguards :   yes   no

safety screen - steam & spill   ☐   ■

water delivery without cup   ☐   ■

spillage container   ■   ☐

splash guards   ☐   ■

used cassettes - hygenic disposal   ■   ☐

_____   ☐   ☐

_____   ☐   ☐

Analysis :   *Improper use by individuals can cause scalding by either late*
placing of cup or premature removal.

Recommendations :   *1. Display clear operating instructions.*
2. Introduce splash guards.
3. Audible/visual warnings.

Actions :   *Review accident record every six months.*

Figure 6.4   Risk analysis

interface is configured the hierarchy is determined; will the equipment be logged to the individual, or will operators be allocated to the equipment register?

Each location will dictate the most logical approach and there may even be a mix between different departments or functions.

The administrative office of a manufacturing complex is more likely to lead with the personnel function and allocate business machines to the individuals, whereas on the production floor the function is primarily performed by the machine and operators are allocated to the equipment.

The real purpose from a facilities management point of view is to achieve the correct location of human and equipment resources with an active database displaying the current status.

6.8   Risk assessment

Health and safety legislation requires active assessment of risk and hazardous operations; it is now necessary to apply risk assessment to all working environments. How does this affect the facilities manager?

The operation of any equipment will, if examined in enough detail, incur some level of risk of personal injury to either the operator or other occupants of the building. Common sense must prevail and many day-to-day activities will not need documenting. The areas of concern are those where there are inherent risks that cannot be totally excluded by automatic safety cut-outs and the like.

The simple office vending machine that allows the operator to place a cup under the hot water supply carries the risk of scalding, clearing paper jams in the photocopier by untrained staff are a burn risk, process equipment involving rollers should not be operated by staff wearing clothing that may become trapped in the mechanism.

These examples are drawn from general office equipment, not specialist processes, so every facilities manager has an interest in risk assessment. The aim must be to site, light, label and service equipment to minimise risk of injury and then to warn, train and restrict operation to contain the remaining risk.

Remember that a fundamental breach of safety through lack of operator awareness of risk is a personal liability on senior management under current legislation. Some company directors have been charged accordingly.

Again, the asset database becomes the ideal place for the facilities manager to log safety and risk information on an equipment by equipment basis. Special requirements, like restrictions only to trained operators, are noted and safeguards to protect the restriction devised. Operation by key is one of the simplest methods of preventing unauthorised operation and, in the event of an accident occurring when physical restrictions have been deliberately circumvented, then management have some defence in the form of operators contributory negligence.

The entire field of health and safety is increasingly complex and the primary responsibility of nominated safety officers, but the facilities manager must be aware of the implications and bear these in mind whenever planning the occupation of a building. The risk assessments with the logged special requirements must be tested against the occupation proposals.

6.9   Multi-location

Organisations with several separate operating locations have further particular problems in asset tracking. We have covered the initial need to log equipment according to location which is workable for items that remain permanently at that location. The complication arises when there is specialist equipment that is not dedicated to a specific location but is moved around on an as-required basis.

Display and marketing equipment like videos, projectors and exhibition stands are examples. The asset-tracking system has two prime functions to discharge, firstly a booking service that co-ordinates the equipment with the time and place of the need, and secondly a tracking record that confirms where the equipment is currently located.

Add to this the logging of personnel responsible for the equipment when out on location and you will have a CAFM register that creates accountability. It is this accountability that makes the system work and minimises costs through loss or damage.

If the equipment in question is a particularly expensive investment, of major strategic importance to the organisation, or in great demand, some companies increase the level of accountability by raising internal rentals for its use. This has the effect of increasing effective usage in high demand situations as no manager wishes to pay more rent from his budget than necessary.

The asset register in these cases will log the rental rates and generate the internal charges based on the advance booking data confirmed by a single documented delivery and return docket system.

6.10   Asset values

As already mentioned, asset registers that replace inventories have a definite role in the accounting and valuation of the business. These values are needed for various functions in the company's accounts; there is the need to evaluate capital allowances accurately, make proper provisions for depreciation and set these calculations over a sensible anticipated equipment lifespan. There is no point in assuming year after year that equipment will last a certain term without reviewing its level of usage. A failure to review can give rise to a premature replacement in accounting terms, which, if the item is costly, can create unexpected and damaging cashflow problems.

The facilities manager by monitoring use against expected life can advise when exceptional provisions should be considered. These provisions may be covered by the business raising finance externally from its bank, leasing company, venture capitalist or shareholders, but in each case advance warning is necessary to set up. It may be appropriate to establish a sinking fund and this route will require greater notice of the event it is intended to cover.

Insurance is the other fundamental use of asset registers; just as it is important not to over-insure and pay excessive premiums, the risks of under-insurance and the application of the principle of average by insurers in the event of a loss can be devastating to a business attempting to re-establish after, say, a major fire.

A comprehensive asset register will avoid the debate over settlement associated with less scientific asset valuations.

7 Life Cycle Costing

7.1 Introduction

In an ideal situation everything in a building falls apart the day after the user has left for the last time and the building is about to be demolished or at least to be substantially refurbished. In common with all ideals the goal is not achievable and we then strive to get ever closer to the perfect solution. This is compromise and the best means of measuring relative success is through cost, a common thread that runs through all aspects of facilities management.

Let us revert for a moment to basics; everything manufactured or constructed has a lifespan, which is governed by many factors, including level of use, durability, quality, climatic conditions and operator skill. The study of lifespan leads to an informed opinion on the life cycle of the item or component. This may be a simple graph showing the item as new progressing through age or use to the point where it is discarded and replaced with new, or may be of a saw-tooth pattern where periodic servicing/maintenance restores peak performance, see Figure 7.1. There will be an economic or practical limit to the number of 'teeth' that a component can be expected to provide and this becomes the life cycle.

The costing element measures the initial capital outlay, amortises it and predicts the recurring maintenance costs to give a projected cost for the component over its life. This projected cost is used to monitor the variance becoming a measure of the component's performance. This cost base draws data from the maintenance function of facilities management and in a CAFM system is an easy discipline of cross-referencing and interrogation of the historic databases.

In long component life cycles the effect of inflation, interest rates and any other external factors that influence the assumptions made when setting out the projected cost are reviewed to update the projected cost. Cost accounting to this standard greatly assists budgeting by creating a control framework, but it is not making full use of the information available.

It is important not to assume that once a life cycle is established it is sacrosanct and can only be reviewed when updating the projected cost; the really useful measure is that of cost–benefit analysis. Cost–

73

PHOTOCOPIER LIFE CYCLE

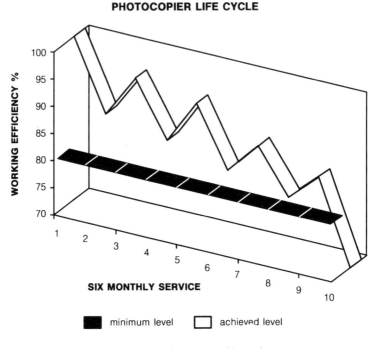

Figure 7.1   Photocopier life cycle

benefit analysis takes this life cycle cost and examines it against alter-native solutions. An example here will illustrate the thinking involved; consider a central heating boiler, for which we have established the lifespan and noted the servicing requirements. Its life is long, up to twenty years, during which time it can be expected to perform within its design tolerances, but will these tolerances look so attractive when measured against newer designs in the last five or even ten years of that life? The facilities manager must keep continually aware of current standards and test existing components through cost–benefit analysis against the alternatives. In our example, with rising energy costs a change of boiler before twenty years will show overall savings if its efficiency shows running cost savings that more than cover the cost of writing off the old boiler over a shorter period and support the amor-tised cost of the new boiler. A simple calculation is shown in chapter 9 to illustrate this point.

Buildings are constructed from a collection of many components, put together with considerable thought in an attempt to match the user's requirements. Traditionally, matters of style, appearance, layout, structural integrity, service requirements and capital cost combine in this thought process to produce the final design. In the last two decades capital cost has gained in prominence, driven by developers' appraisal calculations and the need to show a minimum return on the rental level. The use of full repairing and insuring leases in this country has encouraged the developer to maximise profit at the expense of quality, in the knowledge that once the building is let breakages and replacements are his tenant's responsibility. All too often buildings have been built speculatively or without much dialogue with the final user on the long-term costs associated with the various design decisions. This problem is not inherent where the building owner and user are one. The owner/user, together with the rise of estate managers and now professional facilities managers, are raising the profile of life cycle studies and cost analysis, the outcome of which must be buildings better suited to their purpose.

Originally, life cycle costing was referred to as cost-in-use studies, which might appear more appropriate but fails to encompass initial costs and hence does not embrace the total cost concept. They are the costs incurred in addition to the rent that are a requirement of the lease or necessary to keep the building functioning satisfactorily.

So far we have considered components as individuals but in truth a building has a life cycle. It is an amalgam of all the individual components and, if researched fully, would contain thousands of individual cycles and many dependent interfaces between them. That would be an unworkable situation where research and data collection was absorbing staff resources just for the sake of recording it.

It is necessary therefore to be selective and concentrate on those components of the building that are significant. Cost of the component is an obvious factor, together with its particular demands for servicing or maintenance attention. Other components are selected for study because of their effect on the functioning of the building; this is the strategic importance that has been covered in the chapter on maintenance.

7.2   Use within FM

Life cycle costing is often seen as an exercise only applicable to new construction at the design planning stage. This is true in that major components already incorporated in the construction are unlikely to be replaced, either because the high cost involved renders this uneconomic, or because a fundamental design change would be required.

It is good policy to monitor existing buildings, as there are a number of opportunities available to management to reduce the financial impact of working with less than satisfactory installations. If the occupation is freehold then the most drastic solution is redevelopment; a lesser alternative is a major refurbishment which, if linked to space planning, can often demonstrate a positive cost–benefit.

Assume that you are the facilities manager for an industrial manufacturing unit, and your company has occupied the premises for fourteen years and has a twenty-five year lease. The unit was a speculative development constructed under a fast track design and build contract and now certain deficiencies are apparent in the fabric and services of the building.

There are condensation problems on the roof lining, energy consumption is worryingly high and loading dock doors no longer close properly because of vehicle damage. What can you recommend to your board?

There is a rent review in a year's time and as the landlord is a reputable institution it could be beneficial to open a dialogue linking a refurbishment with the review. Your company may be willing to pay for upgrading the roof insulation to combat the condensation in return for recognition through the rent review that the building had been improved beyond the lease repairing responsibilities.

Perhaps your company's business operates with constant deliveries and despatch, an intensity of use for the loading dock not envisaged at lease commencement and certainly not catered for in the speculative design. An upgrade here with proper accidental damage protection plus perhaps dock sealing will reduce breakages and control heat loss. Again, this is a design improvement which if carried out by the landlord will increase the rent on review. A proper cost–benefit analysis based on both maintenance and life cycle costing data collected by the CAFM system will demonstrate if the energy and repair cost savings at least fund the rent increase.

These examples relate to leasehold property, but the same cost–benefit arguments apply to freehold property, particularly if the facilities manager has organised his workspace costs as described in chapter 3 on space planning. The fact that no identifiable rent exists does not mean that the provision of space is free, so the workspace cost calculations become essential to perform true cost–benefit analysis of improvements.

The prime life cycle function within facilities management is to estimate the useful life and place a cost control on expenditure so that it is controlled within pre-planned budget limits.

There is a reaction to life cycle costing that while attempting to match quality to economic life excessive quality is specified. This is a waste of resources both financial and in the manufacture of the component. Buildings often come to the end of their operative life earlier than originally planned, are demolished and many still serviceable items scrapped or salvaged into the secondhand market.

We are not considering here the major fabric items which usually have a life expectancy in excess of the building's usefulness; the restoration market in the building industry benefits greatly from salvaged materials no longer available new. We are considering services installations that are often so particular to the building that they have either no or minimal residual value; for example, raised access computer floors are expensive new, but worthless on demolition, and there are many items that are just too labour-intensive to dismantle so suffer under the demolisher's ball and chain.

7.3   Data collection

To be useful in management decisions data must be accurate and current. It is also beneficial if it is recorded over sufficient time to demonstrate trends and increase the sampling size sufficiently to produce realistic averages.

So what does this mean to the facilities manager? It means he needs a system that can log and store large amounts of data on his buildings and plant. The storage must then be capable of specific interrogation, so clearly the obvious tools are computer databases. The easiest system to use is the CAFM approach set out in chapter 2. The collation of data is an ongoing process that if kept up to date regularly automatically adjusts to take account of changing circumstances such as market trends, energy costs, insurance costs and more specifically improved core activity processes.

This data collection and analysis will function after a few months' operation but may take some years to produce enough historical information to project future trends. It is this future projection that strengthens the cost–benefit analysis to the point where it can be relied upon for fundamental management decisions.

The alternative is to embark on historical research over perhaps the preceding two years and incorporate the results of that research in the database. As in the case of establishing component life cycles, such an exercise must be selective, and it is the judgement of the facilities manager that sets the priorities. There is no point in researching the roof coverings if they happen to be slate or lead and will outlast the entire building; it is much better to concentrate on lighting, services, lifts, floor coverings and other elements replaceable within the overall span.

As there is a major interdependence on data drawing from the life cycle studies and that from maintenance, it is worth considering running this on a combined basis with defined fields for maintenance functions and others for life cycle. In this way within a facilities management department, where responsibilities are allocated to individuals, the person controlling maintenance is reminded that life cycle costing is relevant to his decision, and vice versa.

7.4   Load monitoring

This chapter has, so far, viewed the life cycle as calendar based, which is appropriate for all the components that deteriorate through age, climatic cycles and attack by atmospheric pollution. There are many components that are subject to all of these factors, plus another, and that is use. Lift systems are a good example of such an installation and is recognisable across many types of buildings. They suffer from age and general deterioration but also wear in direct proportion to their use. A lift that is running all day through demand may spend a high proportion of its life in motion but under a light load, whereas one used infrequently may be subjected to higher working loads and even misuse through overloading. These are factors that must be assessed by the manufacturer or an experienced engineer to establish the wear and tear factor in the life cycle.

Use loadings, where subject to some element of human choice, will vary, so in the case of a lift, a regular measured census of the use and loads is necessary to confirm or update the use profile assumed by the engineer to establish its life.

Lifts are just one example and a walk round any building will show up others; think about the obvious ones like automatic doors, warm-air hand dryers, supermarket checkout desks and also the hidden ones such as drainage pumps.

So now we have a situation where the facilities manager will establish the maximum life cycle of a component under optimum conditions and modify the period to reflect the variables of use and abuse. The cost of the component is linked to the period of use and the projected expenditure is adjusted whenever the period is amended. In practice, some changes in the life expectancy of a component will not come into doubt until a deteriorating expenditure variance is highlighted on the maintenance database. Investigation may then reveal a change of use loading and it is usually only an increase that is noticed.

7.5   Operational requirements

In the chapter on maintenance items of strategic importance are described and there is a responsibility here for the facilities manager not only to avoid unscheduled failures with all the knock-on effects, but also to consider carefully the suitability of the component. Reference to the life cycle set for the component should be matched as closely as possible to the operational requirements. Here he is balancing each strategic component with its alternatives, as a cost–benefit analysis, taking account of life span and overriding operational requirements. The risk analysis of the likely failure of the component needs to meet pre-set criteria from the operational management of the user; any shortcomings on that standard are usually costly, in excess of the savings achieved by lesser performance and they could be disastrous.

7.6   Who provides life cycle cost data?

The data is a blend of information from several sources covering product data, use assessment, projected life and of course cost data.

The product data is collected from manufacturers in the case of factory-built components and from the designers for those elements constructed from site-drawn materials. The designers include architects, engineers both structural and services, interior designers and specialists responsible for IT and communication installations.

The use assessment of active components like lifts, fans and conveyors, is a matter where the facilities manager needs to scrutinise carefully the claims made by manufacturers and then co-ordinate, quantifying the level of use both in terms of continuous or intermittent operation and the loads imposed. With this information the manufacturer or appropriate design consultant will advise on the life cycle.

The cost data for building elements will normally be provided by the quantity surveyor, with further possible input at accountant level on tax and grant statistics that need to become part of the cost–benefit analysis.

The facilities manager must control this process, as data from different sources relating to a single element often conflicts, and it is the facilities manager's function to resolve such conflicts and achieve the correct balance. The lift example used earlier illustrates this point; here the manufacturer will provide life cycle data based on optimum and test programme usage, but this basic load assumption differs from that anticipated or even measured on the lift in everyday use. The facilities manager will, in this case, need to recognise the actual use statistics and modify the manufacturer's predictions.

The basic rule is to look at each component and draw up a list of all sources of informed advice on the component's performance-to-life ratio and then match that advice as closely as possible to actual operating conditions.

7.7   Warranties

Here we are considering component warranties and these can cover plant, equipment and site-built elements of the building.

As the facilities manager, it is your responsibility to ensure that these warranties may be relied upon and do not contain escape clauses that allow responsibilities for performance, durability and reliability to be avoided.

This is a case of checking the long-term stability of the warranty. Remember that such an undertaking from an under-resourced or shell company will be worthless if a significant claim arises. Even warranties purporting to be supported by insurance policies need careful checking to establish in advance of any potential claim that the claim responsibility route and settlement procedures are clear and acceptable. The old adage of read the small print is very appropriate.

One point worth special note is that of transfer of warranties; many guarantors will seek to limit your ability to assign a warranty to a subsequent user of the building and it is important to flag up any such restrictions. It may not be uppermost in the facilities manager's mind when moving into new premises that the company may move on before the premises' life cycle is exhausted, but it is better to secure the transfer option at the outset. Disposal of the premises will be easier if potential new occupiers can recognise the benefit and peace of mind provided by warranties on major components.

Warranties do not just apply to components; they cover services too. The designer of buildings, plant and equipment have a responsibility to fulfil their design briefs and provide a completed building that satisfies the performance standard set by the brief and currently accepted good design. 'Currently' in this context means at the time of the design and construction and is not a guarantee of conformity with future standards.

Again, however, check the small print and the substance of the design consultancy that provides the warranty. In terms of building failure claims, few if any professional consultancy practices will have resources adequate to underwrite the amounts of compensation involved; they will rely on professional indemnity insurance. Such insurance is now compulsory in most building-related consultancy and this is a further safeguard.

7.8   Classification of components

Throughout this chapter components have been discussed without definition of the parts of the building they form. Components may be subdivided into sections, usually referred to as elements and these elements are the principal parts of a building. They are for example:

- External walls including doors and windows.
- Roofs and roof coverings (slates, asphalt, felt, etc.).
- Internal walls, partitions and doors.
- Finishings (plaster, tiling, decorations).
- Services installations (heating, lighting, air conditioning,lifts, etc.).

There are some twenty generally recognised major elements, ranging from the substructure through the external fabric of the building to the internal finishings and furnishings.

It is a convenient framework to use to log all the items of interest in life cycle costing according to these readily understood categories.

There is, however, a further sub-classification within the elements that is of particular interest to the facilities manager, and that is the projected operational life. This classification covers the most durable items like the masonry elements of walls that are expected to last the life of the building, items of intermediate life that will be replaced during the overall life cycle to those that may be considered expendable. It is impossible here to write a definitive list but, as an indication to guide facilities managers, the following is a simplified example:

- Permanent elements — masonry
  — roof structures
  — lead and slate roofs
  — drains
  — roads
- Intermediate elements — boilers
  — pumps
  — lifts
  — floor coverings
  — decorations
- Expendable elements — light bulbs
  — air filters
  — janitorial stores

The intermediate elements are normally programmed for replacement and this programming is set by the life cycle and cost–benefit analysis. Technical advance of new alternative components cannot be ignored and this has already been noted in connection with cost–benefit calculations.

7.9   Leased equipment

Life cycle costing is not restricted to building components. It is very relevant in the control of other equipment including that either purchased outright or leased. Such equipment includes items like photocopiers, printers, vending machines and also tools and plant directly engaged in the business activities.

All items have an economic life and often this is not subjected to an organised objective assessment. It is common practice to replace even relatively costly items through the irritation factor, whereby there is no proper measure of the use level and increasingly unreliable operation or poor quality input prompts purchase giving rise to unplanned expenditure.

Business accounting standards set out rules on depreciation, which is fine for planning against Corporation Tax liabilities and the like, but is seldom used as a prompt to budget for replacement costs.

The gain in popularity of lease purchase arrangements and other such deferred payment methods has encouraged spontaneous purchase, as the immediate cash liability is relatively small but the ongoing liability projects forward over a period of years. It is this ongoing commitment to pay that needs monitoring; it may seem easy to service each lease agreement as they are taken out, especially if several departments or individuals have authority to enter into agreements.

The cumulative effect can prove to be a heavy burden, bearing in mind that long-term debts and liabilities incurred in a good year may need to be serviced in less successful successive years. It is also true that equipment like computers, computer peripherals and telephone/p.a. systems depreciate very rapidly, so there is no residual value to fall back on if the equipment becomes surplus in recessionary times.

The terms of every lease should be examined carefully and attention paid to any penalty clauses that will be activated should you wish to terminate the agreement early.

There are many examples of penal lease break clauses; one of the most common is the case of internal telephone and paging systems. These systems are usually installed in business premises by specialist telephone manufacturers and carry long lease agreements of up to eight or ten years in some cases. The penalty clause for early termination is prohibitive and it is not unknown for businesses moving to new premises having no choice but to install a new system on a new long lease from the same supplier without the ability to choose the best system in terms of both price and performance available on the market.

Check also with leased installations and equipment the terms of ownership and any special requirements for maintenance.

Equipment suppliers are businesses like any other who have the objective to make a profit. That profit can come in two ways, first from the supply of the equipment and then from servicing and supply of consumables. It is a direct parallel with car manufacturers who insist that all servicing must be carried out by a franchised dealer to maintain the warranty; this normally costs more than the local, non-franchised garage.

Copiers and printers fall into this category, with the supplier making a service agreement a condition of the original supply and then making it a condition of the service agreement that they are the only approved supplier of the paper and toner cartridges. At a stroke you have lost the advantages of competition in terms of cost and standard of service.

Before deferred payment purchase plans became so popular funding methods for equipment purchase were simpler. The most basic was to save up and pay cash, not always possible if the item was needed earlier, in which case loans, overdrafts and other cash borrowing was used. The discipline then was to budget for the replacement with a sinking fund that would produce a cash sum when the replacement was purchased. These methods are too simple and would stifle commercial growth in today's commercial environment, but the principle of budgeting for and retaining reserves to cover planned replacement or expansion is sound management practice that will strengthen any company's balance sheet.

Life cycle costing is the key to planning budgeting and the allocation of reserves.

7.10   Quality of product

Some components subject to life cycle control will have a further important factor dictating their useful life. These are components whose operation has a direct effect on the quality of the business's product. They can be climate control items like air conditioners used to maintain the most pleasant working conditions in specific areas of the premises, for deterioration in performance will adversely affect morale and therefore productivity.

Other areas and processes may need clean conditions with all ventilation filtered; a breakdown here could prevent the product quality meeting the customer's standards, at best costly in lost production and wasted materials and probably resulting in a cancelled order.

When assessing components for life cycles the facilities manager should be aware of these special conditions and consider the need to shorten the cycle from that suggested by the component manufacturer or installer to eliminate these risks. This decision should be based on an objective risk analysis that takes account of the views of those responsible for production, customer relations and even sales.

7.11   Value engineering

Value engineering workshops are a common part of the project design development process. The object is to achieve the best possible value for money, in capital terms initially, but to be fully objective the implications of life cycle costs must be taken into account. If life cycle costs are ignored the development team risks influencing the capital cost of the project to the detriment of the whole-life costs. It is essential that the facilities manager is a full member of the value engineering workshop.

These workshops usually take the form of brain-storming sessions attended by all interested parties. The discussion is a continuous process in which all those present can propose changes to the design brief, which are then debated by all the disciplines in the team. The approach is intended to be interactive. The cost of assembling the consultant team and often the preferred contractor for up to a week, usually in a hotel, can easily run to many thousands of pounds, and with most clients adopting a strictly commercial viewpoint attention easily becomes over-focused on the bottom-line capital cost of the project. This is why it is essential that the facilities manager, who will be responsible for the operational costs of the building once it is occupied and in use, is present throughout, in order to ensure a properly balanced appraisal of the traditional development conflict of bottom-line versus whole-life costs.

There is a further issue for the facilities manager to monitor in that the solutions arrived at during value engineering workshops often directly alter the specified components and materials used in the construction; it is therefore essential to have documented evidence that the designer whose specification is altered by the workshop will continue to accept full ownership of the revised design. Failure to note this at the time of the workshop could have serious consequences at a later date in the event of a premature failure or shortcoming in the performance of the building when in use. Without documented agreement, the designer, or more probably the designer's insurers, will seek to avoid any negligence claims on the grounds that their design or specification was compromised at the workshop.

The success of value engineering will depend on the skill and experience of the leader commissioned to run the workshop, together with properly considered terms of reference. The objective of the workshop must be clear from the outset and not just assumed to be an exercise in cost cutting; the goal could justifiably be that of a set economic lifespan for the completed building.

Value engineering is often measured for success before the project commences on site. This is a shortsighted view that fails to measure the real results of the workshop sessions. In order to be comprehensive the benefits identified in the workshops need to be monitored throughout the construction period and the final account costs compared with the predicted costs. If the client is farsighted and has included the lifetime costs in the terms of reference for the overall appraisal, then the monitoring study should be continued after occupation for as long as is necessary to confirm that the expected performance is being achieved.

7.12   Conclusion

Life cycle costing is all about preplanning to anticipate replacement, applying it at the point that is most beneficial to the organisation and ensuring that there are no consequential financial shocks.

As the facilities manager you will not get this correct all the time, but with experience of your building and activities, plus an increasing base of historical data to show trends, the margin of error will reduce to the point where it can be contained within a small contingency budget of, say, five to ten per cent.

Active budget monitoring through expenditure variance reports, presented at least quarterly but preferably monthly, will allow you to seek additional funding before an overspend occurs.

8   Systems and Software

8.1   The dilemma

This chapter looks at the practical selection and use of computer systems in facilities management, setting out guidelines on how to select the most appropriate package for a particular application.

It is the explosion in the everyday use of computers, particularly PCs, that has brought usable software within the reach of any building manager wishing to develop into facilities management. Complex management activities can now be handled by stand-alone PCs costing well under £2000, with software packages ranging from a few hundred pounds to tens of thousands, depending on scope and complexity.

The dilemma facing a new recruit to CAFM lies in the software choice and the claims of the software salesmen. The real tests are twofold: first, will the software do the job required and, second, is its cost in terms of purchase/price, research and data loading costs an ultimate cost benefit to the organisation?

8.2   The system purpose

In our context information technology and computers are not an art form. They are functional devices that relieve us of the drudgery of mass data collection and storage. It is the ability to run extensive databases that accept mass data quickly into a form that allows virtually instantaneous specific interrogation that is the core of CAFM.

The computer application performs three functions:

1. The collection of data

In some cases this is automatic data transfer from other control systems, like building management systems (BMS) and automatic logging systems that measure the use of equipment and plant.

A great deal of data will come from other sources that require definite actions of recording in the CAFM database. Where such data originates in other databases like health and safety or accounts, electronic transfer through computer networks or by floppy disk is to be encouraged on the grounds of economy, speed and accuracy. Every time a human activity is introduced into the chain the risk of error increases sharply and where fundamental information is concerned cross-checking procedures will be needed.

The third source of data is from manual logging and research. This is the most laborious, with the highest risk of input error and is also the most time-consuming. The last factor of time infers cost, depresses the currency of the database and in extreme cases could compromise the overall benefit.

The final source of data is intuitive where interpretation of the visual indexing platform described in chapter 2 generates information on building size, number of rooms, layouts and many other space-related functions. It is a matter of labelling and creating databases to collate information from the computer drawing records.

2. The storage of data

Databases as a medium for information storage have been described in several chapters already. The revolution in CAFM is the ability to store vast amounts of minute detail without overburdening the system. A paper-based, hard copy system is suicidal, self-destructing under the weight of information whereby any hope of retrieving data is lost. Electronic databases are almost limitless in capacity and, through the ability of computers upon a defined command to search the data for matching entries at exceptional speed, the need for finalised filing and indexing associated with hard copy records is avoided.

3. Analysis and retrieval of data

This follows from the storage of data and if we take the asset register as an example we find under furniture that because the asset register replaces the conventional inventory all items are listed by floor and then by room. This is raw data arranged according to a prearranged format set up to ease physical inventory checking while walking round the building. Assume now that this register is being used to order and place furniture in a new building; again the format of floor/room grouping is generated from the computer record; drawing allows proper planning of workspaces and provides delivery instructions within the building.

Say you are the facilities manager overseeing the move and you receive a fax informing you that the manufacturer supplying interview room chairs has had a warehouse fire and cannot meet your delivery deadlines. You need to search the market for an alternative but before this must quickly establish how many units are involved and the budget price allowed in your costings. These chairs are scattered throughout the buildings so on a manual inventory system there is a time-consuming exercise of abstracting and totalling to be done before approaching the market.

On a computer database an interrogation command containing a requirement to match the chair reference will be enough to scan the entire asset register and print an extract report containing a full list of the chairs with locations that can become an emergency market enquiry to alternative suppliers.

The simple analogy is a bucket containing all the door keys for a building individually labelled but thrown in at random. Each can be identified and a specific one can be found given time; but the computer has mastered how to sort through randomly stored data fast and pull out the correct key first time.

8.3   Bespoke systems v. flexibility

There is a fundamental decision to be made very early in the system selection process that concerns the choice of software. Whether to opt for tightly configured programs that are set up to satisfy well-defined facilities management tasks, or to seek more powerful software with a greater degree of flexibility and the ability to adapt to new management demands.

The factors dictating the choice fall into the three categories of staff IT literacy, the degree of definition of the function required and the converse, namely the need for future expansion and flexibility of the system.

The level of IT literacy of the staff who will operate the system, both logging on data and interrogating it to support the facilities management activities, needs to be established, as obviously the more skilled they are in computer and software techniques, the more complex the programs they can operate. Many organisations, however, do not dedicate skilled operators to the facilities manager's support roles and in such circumstances the system has to be user friendly for operation by clerical or supervisory staff.

The tightly configured system suits the latter situation where data in predefined format only is acceptable and reports are similarly generated in predefined form. There is little or no ability to analyse data and interrogate it for other purposes that fall outside the system limits.

Such a system could be one devised to log and report on space allocation in a fully developed building. In this case the building size and layout is static, the variable to be controlled is the allocation of space to either tenants or departments.

The direct management function of recording who is sitting where is completely controlled but any thoughts of using the space data to market test support services of, say, cleaning or maintenance, is beyond the program and the skills of the operators.

The general rule is that the more functions available from the software the more complex are its operations and therefore the higher the grade of operating personnel needed.

In complex premises or estates with large amounts of operational data available it is often best to select the few most pressing management functions to be supported, install a defined system, start logging data and expand the system as confidence grows in its operation and value to the facilities manager. This can be successfully achieved by selecting a specialist facilities management package that is compatible with industry standard architectural CAD software and databases.

It is inevitable that computer-based systems will prove their worth over manual methods through their increased accuracy, vast data storage capacity and speed of response, so the drive towards greater operational flexibility will gather pace.

With powerful, flexible systems the economies of data collection point towards logging all available information on a 'may be useful' basis and harnessing the computer to extract only the relevant data. This approach covers all eventualities on the principle that all the information is in the databases so additional management modules can be created by asking the correct questions and setting up effective data filters. Flexible systems may be operated in three ways:

a)   in-house by specialist departments;
b)   by a specialist FM consultancy;
c)   by a combination of (a) and (b).

The first two options are self-explanatory. The third option (c) relies on the specialist FM consultant to set up and administer the system, providing working modules to their client on a well-defined basis for operation by clerical or supervisory staff. Whenever a request is generated for a new module to satisfy a further function the specialist sets it up from the protected master records and supplies a defined module.

8.4   Selection of systems for in-house use

The choice of hardware is dictated by the eventual choice of software and by far the most common result is from the new generation of fast powerful PCs with the greatest number in the IBM-compatible range. Software is the confusing and occasionally disastrous decision area.

Many bespoke FM systems are generated from small specialist software houses and cautious small suppliers in the IT industry are often full of good ideas that are under-researched with limited application experience in the field. Under-researched and developed systems, together with lack of financial stability, have turned some suppliers into a here-today gone-tomorrow phenomenon leaving their customers without technical back up, program updates or system support. As a cautionary note consider the following points when selecting a CAFM system:

1) Ensure compatibility with industry standard CAD software and databases used predominantly in the design of buildings. A little research will soon demonstrate the market leaders in CAD software, with one in particular standing out as the internationally accepted standard for other systems compatibility.

2) Check the supplier's trading record, seek and take up references, check with other customers referred to in the sales brochures that their use is similar to your intentions and that service has been satisfactory. There are well publicised examples of data handling and management systems set up at great public and corporate expense that do not perform or frequently crash, but for every one of these examples there are many that fall into disuse through inadequate support and obsolescence.

3) Fully define your CAFM brief. Set out the data sources, the input data format, the known retrieval requirements and try to anticipate the future expansion needs. Having done that, ask your proposed software suppliers to meet your brief rather than them

selling you their ideas on what you need. This gives you grounds for comeback should the system disappoint.

4) Seek the advice of an independent FM consultancy that has a track record of setting up systems for clients.

     What is an independent consultancy? It is one with:

     a) no interest in hardware or software sales;
     b) a track record of satisfied clients;
     c) a knowledge of systems available, including their strengths and weaknesses;
     d) the ability to take your brief, develop it, recommend the best software, develop your package, and then debug and install it as fully operational.

     Also check the consultant's professional indemnity insurance cover; it is more reliable in a disaster situation than suing a small software house that may opt to fold leaving you without compensation.

     A consultant with a Quality Assurance registration under ISO 9000 that specifically names facilities management is a worthwhile safeguard.

5) Check out the system costs, not just purchase but including the initial set up, system training, data logging, modular expansion, software updates and technical support charges. Remember that it is easy to make claims for a system's performance and set up plausible demonstrations using the prearranged marketing examples but there is no substitute for using it in anger to show up shortcomings. If these occur during an emergency it is too late and you have made the wrong choice. Choose carefully and establish your line of recourse if your choice lets you down.

9 Worked Examples

9.1 Introduction

This chapter contains some examples of analyses carried out on equipment replacement, outsourcing of services and departmental space budgeting. While the facilities manager will not necessarily be an expert in energy management, fleet operation or space planning, he will be expected to identify and carry out preliminary appraisals on areas of inefficiency that would benefit from a detailed review.

9.2 Component renewal

This is a typical analysis that can be carried out by a facilities manager to establish broad strategy. The example used looks at the cost factors of a boiler renewal.

In the example, an existing boiler installation is examined where the equipment is of an age that suggests it will be significantly less efficient than current boiler technology and therefore may be past its useful life expectancy.

The existing boiler is over ten years old and increasingly inefficient, there are question marks over future reliability and it appears prudent to budget for a replacement.

The factors governing the costs are:
- capital cost of new boiler
- servicing and maintenance
- running costs
- response efficiency

The data is collected and analysed as follows:

Quotation for replacement boiler of equal capacity: £10 000.00

Servicing and maintenance costs over past year
researched from accounts: 1 400.00

Consumption costs researched from accounts: 2 750.00

Estimate of servicing and maintenance costs for
new installation: 500.00

Estimate of consumption costs based on
assumed 20% improvement in efficiency: 2 200.00

The capital cost can be funded at 9% over 5 years raising a repayment charge of £2.14 per month per £100.

$$£2.14 \times 10\,000/100 \times 12 \qquad = \qquad £2\,568.000$$

The increased response efficiency of the new boiler would reduce the running time in each 24-hour cycle allowing a reduction in the start-up period prior to each working day's occupation of the building; assessed as follows:

An 8 hour working day is assumed.
Summer months of May to September impose no heating load, only that of domestic hot water.

On-time of 4 hours per day summer period at a burning proportion of 30% calculates out at running hours of:

$$4 \text{ hrs} \times 109 \text{ working days} \times 30\% \qquad = \qquad 130$$

On-time of 11 hours per day winter period at 65% burning:

$$11 \text{ hrs} \times 151 \text{ working days} \times 65\% \qquad = \qquad 1\,080$$

$$\text{Total running hours per annum} \qquad = \qquad 1\,210$$

New boiler would provide a 20% improvement in the 3 hour daily winter start-up times.

$$3 \text{ hrs} \times 151 \text{ working days} \times 20\% \qquad = \qquad -91$$

$$\text{Total running hours per annum} \qquad = \qquad 1\,119$$

Therefore the improvement in response efficiency is:

$$91/1210 \times 100 \qquad = \qquad 7.50\%$$

These statistics can now be analysed to show if a more detailed appraisal of the options on boiler maintenance or replacement should be commissioned.

ANALYSIS

	Existing Boiler £	New Boiler £	Variance £
Capital cost funded at 9% over 5 yrs p.a.	nil	2 568.00	2 568.00
Servicing and maintenance	1 400.00	500.00	−900.00
Running costs	2 750.00	2 200.00	
Response efficiency adjustment		−7.50%	
	2 750.00	2 035.00	−715.00
	COST per annum		£ 1 781.00

This cost of £ 1781.00 per annum based on simple site observations takes no account of potential tax benefits, increased savings as fuel prices rise and the beneficial reduction in future breakdown risk. All these factors will influence the cost–benefit bringing it closer to the break-even point and then into positive benefit.

The conclusion drawn by the facilities manager in this case should be to investigate the options thoroughly with the help of a services engineer and accountant.

Many support services can be outsourced, as has already been discussed in chapter 5, and this next analysis looks at one such service. The choice of fleet vehicle provision highlights that the range of outsourced services is not restricted to just the most obvious sectors like cleaning, catering, or maintenance but with some lateral thought can be beneficially applied to many other services. This approach to outsourcing is being increasingly driven by organisations' desire to return to core activities, reduce overheads and avoid operating risk from failures in specialist support activities. The failure risk occurs whenever an organisation attempts to provide these activities from within without either the resources or specialist knowledge to run the activity professionally.

9.3   Annual vehicle statistics

Here we have a fleet of fifteen vans operating over varied annual mileages and ranging in age from one to four years. The first chart in Figure 9.1 records age, mileage and analyses downtime per vehicle per 1000 miles of use.

The facilities manager needs to establish an optimum level of downtime and in this case has used the best average for each vehicle age group, i.e. 1.24 for four-year-old vans, 0.92 for three-year-old, 1.17 for two-year-old and lastly 0.71 for the youngest in the fleet.

The analysis graph then sets a maximum barrier above which performance is unacceptable; in this case an allowance of + 25% on the optimum time is used and it becomes clear that eight vehicles, or more than half of the fleet, are underperforming, so a doubt now exists about the efficiency of the distribution fleet.

The second table in Figure 9.2 records the activity profile of each van, allocating time into categories of running, standing and down time to produce an activity ratio for each by comparing the net standing time with running time. A definition of running and standing time is necessary to understand the analysis; running time includes all periods during which the vehicle is in use delivering, loading and unloading. Standing time covers periods of inactivity like overnight parking and time awaiting instructions.

In this case there is no calculated optimum use ratio and in this example the facilities manager or the transport manager has set a target of 60% as the optimum. The chart shows that four vans are exceeding the target, one is meeting it and ten are falling short.

Armed with these statistics the facilities manager could now prepare an enquiry document inviting external fleet operators to bid for this work. The enquiry would invite prices on an all-inclusive rate to be charged to include down time at the operator's risk. Adequate back-up resources and pre-agreed response times for additional vans would eliminate a large proportion of the standing time and encourage proper planning of distribution programmes. A significant cost saving is possible in this case, with the added benefits of transferring the operating risk to the fleet contractor and, if the fleet charges were then allocated to cost centres, economic load volumes and full use of vehicles would be encouraged through the incentive on managers to minimise costs accruing to their cost centres.

RECORDS			DOWNTIME				
VAN ref	AGE yrs	ANNUAL MILES	SRVCE hrs	BRKDOWN hrs	ACCIDENT hrs	TOT hrs	AV per 1000 mls
1	4	18600	11	35	0	46	2.47
2	4	12300	8	22	0	30	2.44
3	4	22200	16	31	55	102	4.59
4	4	153000	11	8	0	19	1.24
5	3	7600	3	4	0	7	0.92
6	3	26500	22	22	0	44	1.66
7	3	15000	11	8	60	79	5.27
8	3	15800	11	5	0	16	1.01
9	3	14100	8	9	0	17	1.21
10	3	8900	3	11	0	14	1.57
11	2	13900	8	6	37	51	3.67
12	2	16300	11	8	0	19	1.17
13	2	16100	11	3	122	136	8.45
14	1	15600	11	0	0	11	0.71
15	1	15100	11	2	0	13	0.86

FLEET MILES	233300		TOTAL DOWN TIME		604
			AVERAGE DOWN TIME		2.59

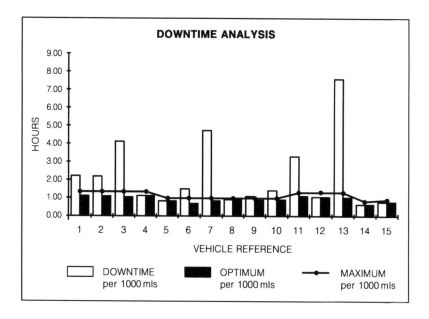

Figure 9.1   Annual vehicle statistics

VAN ref	RUNNING TIME hrs	STANDING TIME (all) hrs	DOWN TIME hrs	STANDING TIME (net) hrs	ACTIVITY RATIO %
1	715	1205	46	1159	61.69
2	473	1447	30	1417	33.38
3	693	1227	102	1125	61.60
4	588	1332	19	1313	44.78
5	42	1878	7	1871	2.24
6	736	1184	44	1140	64.56
7	618	1302	79	1223	50.53
8	632	1288	16	1272	49.69
9	671	1249	17	1232	54.46
10	370	1550	14	1536	24.09
11	515	1405	51	1354	38.04
12	709	1211	19	1192	59.48
13	596	1324	136	1188	50.17
14	821	1099	11	1088	75.46
15	679	1241	13	1228	55.29

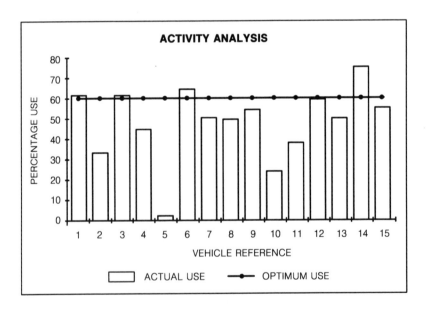

Figure 9.2   Vehicle activity profile

9.4   Workspace cost calculation

The assessment of workspace costs like those shown in Figure 3.1 are the result of statistical analysis of actual costs. This next example shows how the chart in chapter 3 was researched; obviously every building and even differing uses of parts of the building will generate different results, but this one relates to a floor in an office building of 2500 square feet at a rental of £12.

		£	%
Rent 2 500 @ £12	=	30 000	32
Rates allocated from the overall charge equate to	=	21 000	22
Energy consumption is again allocated from the overall charge	=	3 175	3
Servicing includes cleaning, consumable supplies (tea, coffee and any other ancillary function necessary to support working operations).			
Cost researched from accounts and actual amounts paid	=	9 150	10
Circulation looks at the movement space necessary within the net lettable space including corridors and traffic routes, communal areas like refreshment points and staff rooms, and meeting rooms for general intermittent use.			
In this case circulation is measured as 780 sq. ft. which at £12	=	9 360	10

Surplus space evaluates single occupation of double or triple space rooms, the use of non system or co-ordinated furniture and low density occupation. The last two parts are related and to quantify the waste first design an ideal workstation from scratch then arrange the required number on the floor in a space planning exercise to achieve the maximum density compatible with good working.

The space released is classified as surplus.
The total assessed in this case
was 985 sq. ft. at £12   =   11 820   13

Furnishing includes the cost of all soft,
movable and built-in furnishings, screens and
demountable partitions converted to an
annualised cost necessary to create an
adequate replacement sinking fund and costs
                                           =   9 150   10

	Totals	93 655	100

Using this example at the bottom end of the workspace cost ratio range it becomes obvious that workspace in this office building has a true cost of £37.46 per square foot.

An immediate review of costs will show a benefit with a reduction in space used that will create a saving in rent and rates immediately, assuming that the space can be returned to the landlord or sub-let and an attack on the surplus space which at 985 square feet in this case amounts to over 39% of the total floor area will increase efficiency, create order and more than cover any reorganisation costs through the savings.

Remember that these are savings in revenue costs, so they are repeated annually while the corrective measures remain in force.

10 Services

10.1 Introduction

In the context of property, services means heat, light, power to most people and with some thought would also include communications like telephones. This chapter will consider all of these from a facilities management point of view, plus other less obvious installations.

The approach to the practical management of services is dictated by the type of building, its use and age. The type of building and use are directly related and, in terms of services, the difference in priorities between highly complex installations like hospitals or laboratories and simpler uses in warehouses make it necessary to assess the strategic importance of the services functions at each installation to establish the facilities management controls. The age of the building is important as generally in existing buildings the services if installed as a retro-fit process will be a compromise set to achieve acceptable working performance. In new purpose-designed accommodation the services will still be a compromise but to much finer tolerances and therefore with a higher degree of functional attainment.

All these problems are services design factors and the facilities manager's interest is to influence the design brief whenever possible to ease the operational requirements. What this really means is that it is better to design in operational functions like maintenance, access and standby equipment, rather than, as all too often happens, attempt to fit the restrictions imposed by the operation of the building round an existing installation. The access to equipment for maintenance purposes has already been covered in detail in chapter 4.

The problems and priorities in each installation will be different, but the goal is universal in achieving acceptable performance in use.

10.2 Cable management

Traditionally, buildings in the UK built for tenanted occupation have not been pre-wired, so the cabling has been carried out as part of the fitting-out works at the tenant's expense. This differs from the approach in other countries where higher levels of distribution cabling are normally built in. There are arguments for and against both approaches; with the basic landlord's shell the capital cost of the development is less, allowing a more competitive rent, but longer rent-free periods are demanded by the tenant for fitting out. The advantage to the tenant is the option to take on a completed building and wire specifically to suit his occupation pattern. Buildings with cabling built in need to anticipate the eventual occupation and wire accordingly; this will work whenever a pre-let is in place and the occupier can provide details of his requirements, but otherwise will duplicate effort by parallel routing whenever the landlord's wiring does not satisfy the user requirements. The temptation is to use or adapt what is there rather than installing the correct distribution, which leads to inefficiency and operational unreliability.

Cable management is probably the most difficult function for the facilities manager to control, especially in buildings with a high incidence of occupational churn. He is expected to have anticipated every possible use of the space and have all cable systems installed for instant connection to the occupier's equipment. This is significant, bearing in mind that equipment requirements in this context include communications, telephone and computer networks, power, light, intercom, emergency uninterrupted power supply (UPS), data and other facilities.

Starting at the beginning, the design of cabling layouts is the basis of subsequent management, as it creates the record platform showing both schematically and in location plan form the layout and availability of wired services throughout the building. A CAFM system is ideal for recording this information and is easily revised as the system develops to cater for the occupation of the building. As new cable runs are added they are logged to the record, and the interface with a database records the users, loads and network security.

The purpose of cable management is to know what is available in the building, where it is and the load capacity of each circuit or network. Safety and security are other considerations to be monitored. As an example, suppose there is a piece of electrical equipment essential to the operation of the building that is important enough to require a fallback position with a standby unit that can be activated if the mainstream equipment fails. If the failure is within the equipment then the standby is activated. If, however, the failure is in the power or control circuits then to be effective the standby unit must be driven from a separate circuit. This may seem obvious, especially to engineers designing the original installation; the risk arises when standby equipment is installed at a later date, often by contractors who were not involved with the original installation or do not understand the significance of the back-up. Without proper instruction and cable management controls a circuit failure can render the mainstream unit and the back up inoperative through this one fault.

Additions and alterations to cable distribution are inevitable to accommodate use changes in the building. Occupational churn, expansion and contraction with market conditions, new equipment and business systems all make cable management a complex and moving target.

Security needs to be addressed just like safety; power circuits, for example, should not be arranged to allow general disruptions through malicious tampering or vandalism and data circuits need to be graded for security and confidentiality of information. Cable management in this case needs to track the connections to the networks, locate the system blocks that restrict access and, in the event of a breach of security, identify all individuals and terminals with approved access to the data.

The distribution of cabling throughout a building is designed to suit the occupancy; it should also have the flexibility to cope with change, without involving major building works and, to achieve this, factors, like zoning, programmable controls and location within the structure are important.

Zoning is an obvious approach; it helps to control load, helps to isolate problems and allows sub-tenant/departmental cost accounting and charging. In a speculative office block zoning may be by floor to allow separate metering in multiple occupancy. Zoning allows areas to be isolated and activated without disrupting the entire building; this is useful if a shutdown is needed to carry out maintenance or alterations.

Programmable controls for lighting, heating, ventilation and power are gaining in popularity as they allow the availability of services in the building to be set up at will by a central computer-based programmer. Programmable controls are useful in buildings that are accessed by key staff at non-regular times of day or night. If for example the building contains a computer suite that key individuals can access 24 hours a day but are to be restricted to that area only outside normal working hours, then programmable lock suiting will physically restrict access; also, programmable light and data switching will deny unauthorised access and can be used to supplement intruder systems in detecting security breaches. There are economy grounds for programmable controls in that lighting and power can be shut down on a pre-arranged pattern that does not restrict operations but saves energy consumption.

Lastly, the location within the building offers a choice; in new offices cable runs can be underfloor, in ceiling voids or around the perimeter. The final choice will depend on the amount of open plan space or cellular offices envisaged and the design of workstations. Some workstations attempt to provide a micro-climate for the individual so are heavily serviced. They are more difficult to move than unserviced desks, but in the space planning context they are free from the restrictions of space-based heating and ventilation. The simple desk that does not incorporate heating and ventilating terminals is therefore more portable as it needs fewer service connections and those that it does need are more flexible, usually being wiring for power and communications and not ductwork. Space planning, workstation design and the ratio of open-to-cellular occupation will influence the cable run locations with the ultimate consideration of accessibility for maintenance.

There is cable management software now available that can track the physical location of individual equipment, log its use and monitor the data accessed. The use of this technology sets up smart zones which provides a useful control over key or sensitive areas.

The cable networks to be managed are varied; they include light, power, data, communications, peripheral networks and control circuits.

10.3 Zoning and distribution

The tracking of cables has already been discussed under cable management, so here we will look more closely at the facilities management requirements for zoning and distribution. The application is to all services used regularly throughout the premises and the purpose of zoning and distribution is to provide adequate supply to service the design load. Without zoning, distribution would in its simplest form be on the 'hub and spoke' principle where a cable is run from the source to each point of use. The first refinement is to introduce a distribution ring, either allowing access directly at point of use, or through short spur circuits. This is practical only in the smallest installations; most houses for example have more than one ring. As buildings get bigger more distribution zones are used; these allow isolation of areas and separate metering but also reduce the load on each distribution ring, thereby also reducing the weight of cable needed. The safe use of lighter weight cable makes installation easier using smaller conduits and trunking.

Zoning with a control system is of use whenever load sharing or shedding is necessary, for example in power failure situations where emergency back-up is used to keep essential services running.

Programmed zoning is used to stagger start-up loads where an entire complex coming on line at, say, 9 a.m. would create a major surge in demand and the peak can be smoothed by controlled switch on. Some electricity accounts are adjusted according to the highest load recorded in the cycle, so staggered start-up shows economies.

10.4 Power and light

The facilities manager's interest in power supply within the premises concerns the availability of adequate service to allow the expected activities to be accomplished. It is not his responsibility to design the power services, but whether installing a new distribution or altering an existing one the designer needs a brief that sets out the performance requirements. The facilities manager is thus the focusing point that co-ordinates the production demands with the supply of support services like power.

The activities envisaged in the premises will dictate the load and the equipment to be driven will define the need and location of any phased power.

It will always be prudent to build in some spare capacity for future expansion or to accommodate replacement equipment which, in a modernisation programme, will often have a higher work rate or perform additional tasks, probably with the penalty of a greater load. Power requirements range from simple domestic systems using 13 amp sockets to three phase for industrial and manufacturing processes.

There are other specialist power needs and, with the increasing dependence on information technology systems within the business's core activities, controlling the building and the working environment and of course in security, the need for uninterrupted power supplies (UPS) becomes essential. The facilities manager must be aware of all equipment in the building that will put lives, security business data and the like at risk in a power failure situation. UPS systems provide a practical solution, particularly to preserve data in IT systems, but if the requirement demands support of power beyond emergency levels, then a stand-alone source will be necessary. Standby generation using diesel- or gas-powered units that are either activated automatically or manually may be large enough to support the total demand until such time as the utility service is restored. Premises that justify such measures will also demand that the standby equipment is reliable; the facilities manager therefore needs to define the responsibility for servicing and test running, to delegate the task and to verify that it is discharged properly.

Light shares many of the challenges of power management and the facilities manager again needs to coordinate the user demands with the system design. The main difference between the two is that, while power supplies the energy to accomplish tasks, lighting is an environmental service that makes the workplace capable of occupation. It is therefore necessary to ensure that lighting intensity and glare control are matched to the activities being performed, a point to note carefully whenever an internal reorganisation takes place that changes the use of a space. Buildings that experience high levels of occupancy place demands on the flexibility of lighting. Some offices in activities like financial services, banking and insurance fluctuate in the mix of departments so frequently that a rigid lighting system, requiring revision before moves can be completed, will seriously inhibit the users' occupation of the building. This problem is most obvious in space like a banking dealing room that is often deep in its range extending far from natural lighting and is therefore dependent on artificial illumination. The use of VDU screens dictates light intensity levels which can be critically upset by a department change that requires a revised partition layout. There is no complete answer, but imaginative design using programmable switching of zoned lighting will compensate for many use changes.

The ability to add further luminaires on a plug-in modular basis or incorporating progressive switching into the existing luminaires allows the light level to be adjusted up and down as necessary.

The building services engineer will control the programming but the facilities manager will be ultimately responsible to senior management for the provision of effective workspace that creates efficient working conditions and satisfies the legislation.

As lighting is essential to building occupation, emergency lighting is a safety requirement that must be monitored by the facilities manager. Whether the system be battery supported or driven off standby supplies, it must be adequate to serve the current use of the building and be tested regularly.

While much thought goes into the internal lighting system, external requirements like floodlighting and security lighting are also important. External lighting can be expected to meet several criteria; it can be a marketing banner drawing attention to the building itself or its function; it can also be for safety purposes easing access to and from and around the building; finally good lighting is a major security factor.

All the information needed for easy reference on power and lighting installations is stored on a CAFM system with databases driven to manage the installation. These databases can be configured to show the location of outlets, the available load capacity on any zone or circuit, the current lighting programme and finally will monitor energy consumption through the BMS. The energy consumption statistics build into an historical data analysis of the building's performance where fluctuating demands should correlate with ups and downs of activity. Careful scrutiny of consumption graphs will show patterns that identify seasonal variations, leaving any other deviations from the expected profile exposed and open to scrutiny. Over a period of time, say two to five years, the control of energy wastage and the refinement of the BMS should more than fund the cost of implementing the controls.

This feedback will also act as a confirmation for any cost–benefit used to support the installation of more energy efficient equipment. Chapter 7 on life cycle costing dealt with cost–benefit analysis in considerable detail.

10.5 Telephones and communications

Services in this part include voice and data transfer, both internally and externally, and it is the facilities manager's responsibility to know the routes and location of all cable and optical fibre runs. Flexibility to accommodate change or expansion is expected but there are other considerations specific to this type of cabling.

Confidentiality is the most obvious need, applying to both voice and data networks. Intercepted telephone conversations are a fact, the most personal can become public knowledge if the media become interested, but the real danger is of commercial damage with company data passing to third parties. Data protection is even more critical, largely because of the speed of transfer whereby entire confidential databases can be copied and transmitted virtually instantaneously. So what are the safeguards and how does the facilities manager fit into the scene? The facilities manager will not necessarily be an expert on IT, but he will need to be familiar with the data networks and specifically who has access to them and who has not. The IT planning will set up networks with varying degrees of access; for example, a company employing electronic mail to pass internal messages from terminal to terminal will make it available throughout the organisation, even linking geographically remote locations.

The security of any confidential information passed by this means is a matter for the management procedures of the company to control, with responsibility placed on the individuals using the system to conform. Security risks can be substantially reduced by restricting some networks on a need-to-know basis. Here the IT manager will be advised of groups of people that need to share data and all others will be barred from access. This is not a problem until some of the restricted access individuals move their working location; the network must then be reconfigured to maintain their continuity and deny any access to their vacated workstation. The facilities manager needs to coordinate the changes and amend his master record.

Data networks can be further secured by restricting the access times to prevent out-of-hours interrogation. Telephone networks are programmable in a similar way with levels of call barring available to control both use and cost.

Hard-wired circuits are the traditional approach to communications, but there are alternatives that the facilities manager should remember. Satellite and microwave transmission for external communications, radio links for communications internally and in the immediate environs and, as an alternative to metal-cored cable, optical fibre is gaining in use. Optical fibres have a distinct advantage in complex systems with many users accessing great volumes of data. The use of decoders to select the appropriate pulses from a multi-use core allows the simultaneous transmission of different data strains with the appropriate messages received by each terminal. The reduction in cabling bulk is an advantage for the physical installation and the data security aspect is controlled by the decoder availability; without the correct decoder the data cannot be accessed.

10.6 Security systems

Intruder systems, whenever installed to protect the premises both inside and outside, are managed by the facilities manager; he needs to know the areas covered by the systems, the level of security attained and any restrictions placed on the free entry and exit from protected areas. It is the end function of the systems that interests us, as does the use of physical controls, like keypad locks, swipe cards and other smart systems that differentiate between authorised and unauthorised personnel that must be logged to the CAFM system. Current generations of security locks are programmable, with keys or card entry that may be set up with commands recognised by the lock that restrict entry by time and date or even prohibit entry during external events like security or fire alerts. The benefit of such systems applies to multiple key user installations or where access is to be allowed to individual personnel for a limited period; in these situations the keys or cards can be deactivated by instructing the lock to refuse entry. It can also be a useful function to prevent entry by former staff without the delays and difficulties of recovering keys. Lost or stolen keys can be rendered useless in a similar way.

The complexity of intruder and access limiting systems will be dictated by the needs of the premises and the sensitivity of the activities performed there, but remember that it is easy to become over-sophisticated and it will be the facilities manager's role to match the building user's needs to the most appropriate installation. The control of the system depends on the complexity and required response time to an activation. Simple systems are set and disarmed locally and usually rely on lights and sounders to warn of an incident; the hope is twofold, to scare off intruders and to summon a security inspection. As systems become more complex, it is increasingly necessary to opt for central control and monitoring, either by a fully manned control room on site or through a security link to a remote station. The management of centrally controlled systems falls to the security officer, but the facilities manager has an interest in monitoring the performance of any outsourced services. These services will include reviewing independent security firms operating remote control rooms on a bureau basis and the response times from an alarm activation to investigation on site.

The final addition to intruder security systems is the use of closed circuit TV as both a deterrent and an instant window into the critical area; the logging of cameras and their field of view should be to the CAFM system. This allows existing coverage to be examined and modifications planned as part of any use rationalisation of the premises.

Entry and exit screening is useful in tracking the occupation of a building, as it will provide instant occupation counts by logging all individual entries and departures. Good building management and greater requirements of Health and Safety make it increasingly important to know how many people are in the building and, if a zoned screening system is used, where those people are. Emergency evacuations of large or complex premises are more efficient with an instant check for unaccounted occupants. Whenever such a system is likely to be used in emergency procedures the control room needs to be in a secure location and a secure power supply must be available. There is no point in having such a system if the emergency that triggers its use also causes the system to crash.

The security of company data has already been covered under cable management, but a more practical application of security systems is in the monitoring of critical process environments. Some processes are temperature critical, others require monitoring to warn of health and accident hazard risks. The design of such systems is a specialist service not usually within the facilities manager's expertise, but nevertheless he will need to know of their existence and function and who is responsible for their proper operation. Alarms in general fall into this category, including fire/smoke detection, leakage and health hazard warnings. The maintenance, testing and safety check records are best coordinated and held by the facilities manager on the databases driven by the CAFM system.

The final security systems considered here concern the isolation or correction of an incident. Fire is the most obvious emergency, where sprinklers or automatic fire control equipment are available to contain the outbreak and bring it under control. The measures used in addition to fighting the fire directly concentrate on safety by containing the spread and creating safer escape routes. The management responsibility is to ensure the correct maintenance and testing of equipment so that it can be relied upon to perform in the event. Automatic shutters and fire doors must work and regular checks to confirm they have not been wedged or tied open seem obvious, but often they are seen as inconvenient obstructions during normal working and, ironically, a convenient fire extinguisher is often used as a door stop. Automatic process shutdown procedures, together with fuel cut-off valves are there to minimise any incident, and again they need to be logged and checked as part of the FM system.

10.7 Pipework

Heating, cooling, hot and cold water are all common pipework installations in buildings. They are not attractive visually, so great efforts are made during design to conceal them within the structure or behind finishings and this causes endless problems whenever a leak is to be traced. Leaks also have a tendency to travel both vertically and horizontally, appearing some distance from the source fault. Without proper logging of pipe runs, investigation can be a damaging process as the leak is traced back to source. The damage is physical to the finishings and also to profitability through disruption of the business activities. It is the task of the facilities manager to respond quickly and efficiently to such emergencies.

Obviously, the goal must be to achieve accurate logging of pipe runs and proper labelling of the pipes for contents, flow direction and pressure warnings, plus tracking activities, with progressive isolation of the faulty system leaving as much of it operational as possible. A fully logged system on CAFM will show the isolation options that can be used to stop the flow and so narrow down the area of search for the fault.

As an illustration of the problem consider a leak in the domestic cold water supply from a roof storage tank occurring at fifth floor level, but only becoming apparent as ceiling dampness two floors lower. Tracing up through two floors will be disruptive; it will be much better to open a small section of the damp ceiling and progressively shut down the supply floor by floor until the flow stops, then go directly to the identified level and make the repair.

10.8 Ductwork and ventilation

The principles of logging pipe runs applies to ductwork, with the additional need to log the terminal or diffuser locations for integration with future changes to internal partitions, the location of the fire stops and, if a condensation risk occurs, the methods used to prevent the build up of trapped water.

Occupational churn within a building causes supply and balancing problems with ducted heating or ventilation systems. Altered partition layouts upset the cellular to open space mix, and equipment levels increased or reduced from the original design parameters change the equipment gain loadings. The system will probably need some rebalancing, a point to remember whenever moving departments around.

Whenever looking at operating and energy costs, the use of heat recovery and the balance of recycling with fresh air mix reduces the amount of waste heat discharged externally, thereby increasing energy efficiency and reducing overhead costs. Changing use patterns of the buildings can allow a beneficial adjustment to heat recovery and conservation.

10.9 Intelligent buildings

This is a term in common use for some time on occasions by designers attempting to talk up their buildings but more recently the growth and availability of usable IT systems has made a true interpretation of the intelligent building possible.

The growth of communication systems that monitor the performance aspects of a building's functions, like its environment of heat, light, ventilation, together with ever improving BMS, has created buildings that react to changing circumstances and seek to maintain the designed environment throughout seasonal, time and occupational variations.

The intention, as with all facilities management, is to provide unhindered workspace that encourages a feeling of well-being in the occupants and therefore fosters the highest levels of productivity.

The advent of powerful usable computers, especially PCs, make this possible by programming as many services functions as possible to meet the occupancy over the building's useful life. The useful life will be a period long enough to satisfy the investment criteria in the services, and BMS, and produce an overall beneficial return to the occupier.

The current computer trap is in the choice of software, where uniform standards for compatibility have still to emerge. It is therefore essential whenever specifying equipment that will be monitored by the building's BMS to state clearly the compatibility with the control systems.

Configuring a BMS is a specialist task but in order to brief the designer fully the functions that are expected need to be defined. The facilities manager can assist here by compiling a 'wish list' from the department managers. This list will inevitably exceed the practicalities of the system, but is the starting point for editing down to an acceptable list of effective requirements. These are then relayed to the system designer as his brief.

One of the strengths of intelligent buildings is the ability to sense when the building is occupied or empty and switch up or down the supporting services; many systems can, for example, default to a stand-by mode overnight, being reactivated on a time trigger or by reoccupation the next day. Obviously, some systems like heating have a response time, so they need to be activated in advance of the day's occupation whereas lighting can be considered an instant response controlled by people sensing. All these intelligent systems minimise energy demands and therefore cost.

A growing concept in building occupation, particularly in large offices, is that of flexible working. The practice of staggered working hours for staff has existed for years and has exaggerated the impression of unused non-productive space throughout the building. The latest approach is to design the internal layouts to accommodate the expected peak occupancy of the building. The peak occupancy is less than the total staff numbers, as at any time a proportion will be out on business, off sick or on holiday, at which times their desks will not be earning for the company. A few forward-thinking companies have explored desk-sharing culminating in the provision of standardised workstations that are not allocated territorially to individuals. Anybody coming to work finds a vacant workstation, logs on to the communication and data networks and uses that space for as long as their tasks demand. Standardisation is the key to success, as each workstation must provide identical services like telephones, intercom and computer terminals. The supporting service networks need to be intelligent and log the individual's identity so that they may be tracked and located for incoming communications. The economic arrangement supports this approach in organisations with a mobile workforce, like financial services or marketing departments, where much business is conducted outside the office. It is possible to service three, four or even five individuals with just two workstations with an obvious benefit in furniture, equipment and office space costs.

A spin-off benefit is that a cleared desk regime must operate as an individual cannot assume that he will occupy the same place the next day, so tidiness improves and central filing systems are effective.

There are disadvantages with flexible working; most significantly the reaction of the individuals who can experience a feeling of insecurity without a regular workstation and, while communication and data access can be achieved by logging on, departments providing support services, like secretarial, can find it difficult to locate people who have become moving targets.

The use of IT networks, electronic mail and networked memo pads overcomes the tracking problem and in turn reduces the hard copy paper in circulation internally. The reduction in paper use brings benefits through reduced copying costs, reduced refuse collection and disposal volumes and a reduced fire risk.

10.10   Central stations

We have already looked at the use of central controls in security systems and in the building management functions, so here we now look at the function and future development of the control centre. The idea that all systems in a building can be controlled from one computer-driven nerve centre adapting to minute-by-minute demands and providing accurate up-to-date operational data is already available at a price. The progress in software development is significant in raising the friendliness of any system and making it accessible to non-computer technical managers. The increasing use of such a system, through the latest developments in Windows-type programs and the downloading of performance data into database spreadsheets like Excel or Lotus 1-2-3, allows much more management awareness of running costs. The allocation of costs to cost centres or departments further devolves the incentive for efficient use of the building and is a key item in performance-related pay calculations.

It is the choice and design of central stations that will dictate the software compatibility requirements for the installed services equipment. The facilities manager's interests here include not only the ability to download current and historical performance data to spreadsheets for analysis, but also to achieve compatibility of VDU screen interfaces.

There is nothing more irritating than being unable to configure a data display knowing the information is all there waiting to be viewed.

10.11 Waste disposal

The cleaning and collection of rubbish is a support service carried out either by staff or by outsourcing. We are not concerned here with these operational services, but we are concerned with the type of waste generated, its disposal and particular restrictions.

Waste that cannot be disposed of by local authority services usually comes from security-sensitive sources, is contaminated, or is a health hazard. Each of these categories presents a problem to the facilities manager; sensitive material may need shredding, incinerating or even disintegrating. The particle size necessary to protect the confidentiality will dictate the method chosen, also acknowledging that some items cannot safely be burnt and others will damage disintegrator plant. There is the choice of on-site disposal or removal by a specialist off site and EC regulations are becoming increasingly strict about disposal methods.

Incineration is the most common method of dealing with volume and large on-site facilities generate heat that can be tapped to reduce the bought-in energy requirements. A secure route and storage of material for destruction will be needed, together with a system to filter out waste that would create a hazard if burnt. Pressurised containers and even fire extinguishers have found their way into incinerators with disastrous consequences.

If you are planning a disposal facility consider the following:

- Volume and combustibility of waste.
- Potential by-product energy contribution.
- Volume and disposal of residual material (ash).
- Environmental restrictions.

The disintegrator method grinds the waste into an undecipherable mass, but the equipment is susceptible to damage from hard material like metals, bricks and the like. The residual volume is greater than with incineration but may have a scrap value for recycling or as a fuel for boilers.

Follow the previous guide points, eliminate the inappropriate methods, and then carry out a cost–benefit analysis on the remaining options.

10.12 Cost accounting

Any facilities manager will try to achieve the most cost-effective solution to a task and with services the need is to monitor consumption, in both volume and cost, then compare the current figures with historical data from previous years. Trend analysis is an accurate method of measuring the overall effectiveness of changes and improvements.

Consumption may be the largest annual cost of services, but control of maintenance is important to analyse breakdowns. Remember the knock-on effect of lost production should be linked into the breakdown costing to provide true figures for cost–benefit analysis of proposed equipment upgrades.

The tenant or departmental billing option that charges out services costs can be set up on an individually metered basis, or by applying a researched service charge over each category of space use, or by monitoring services costs and allocating them according to recorded departmental demand over the charging period. This final level of monitoring acts as a check on the metering by the public utilities and therefore their charges.

Telephone charges are controlled by call logging, whereby individual handsets or departments can have all calls made listed and costed. The effect of this is twofold in management terms; calls become shorter and at lower charge periods and the proportion of personal calls declines.

10.13 Specialist services

Industrial and medical gases are specialist installations that require logging of pipe runs, plus clear identification of contents and location of controls or fittings. Testing programmes are required to verify supply quality by sampling and checking delivery flows or pressures. It is the facilities manager's responsibility to organise and delegate these tasks to suitably qualified people, then maintain the records of the verification results. Leakage testing not only reduces waste, but avoids potential hazards through atmospheric contamination.

The location and serviceability of connection points to these installed systems is important if the workspace is to operate at best efficiency, so knowledge of the existing system held on CAFM allows immediate graphical reference. Any alterations to the system to make the distribution and access more convenient can be trial tested in the computer model, with checks on adequacy of distributed capacity.

Steam distribution and vacuum services are generally process-linked and require controls on safety testing. The testing programme is best monitored by the facilities manager using in-house personnel or through outsourcing and term contracts. Whichever route is followed a clear brief, of the tasks to be performed, of corrective action to be taken, and of the reporting procedures, will be written by the facilities manager.

There are other specialist services demanded in buildings to support the core activities; for example, compressed air occurs in industrial processes, often as a safe means of driving hand tools. Power may be required at special voltages; so, in a complex services installation the facilities manager will be logging a CAFM record of all the cable and pipe paths, with identified isolation procedures that can be activated rapidly in an emergency or applied in a controlled manner to allow system maintenance or modification.

With all this data available graphically on-site, building and floor plans, together with the linked databases, the use of services will become progressively more efficient, the costs will be controlled and downtime will be minimised.

11 Allied Activities

11.1 Introduction

As part of the constant effort to improve the use of buildings, it is worthwhile to take account of a whole range of peripheral activities. Quality Assurance schemes have been in existence for many years but are now gaining widespread recognition as a powerful management tool. The available range of expert advice on procurement methods for building works, together with the use of external consultants, often present the facilities manager with a bewildering choice. The optimum point at which to commission a project manager to assume the day-to-day control of capital works can be difficult to recognise and can be disastrous if overlooked.

Organisation and method (O&M) studies, when properly defined and researched, are a prime source of data. It is worth dealing with each of these activities in a little more detail.

11.2 Quality assurance

Quality Assurance to the familiar BS 5750, now replaced by the ISO 9000 international standard, if properly constituted, is not simply a marketing device but a discipline that strives towards providing an expected standard. The following quotation from an accredited company's quality policy statements sums up the objective . . . 'to supply services and products to the correct quality and to be able to ensure that client requirements are met'.

The key to a successful quality system is in the interpretation of correct quality; this does not necessarily mean the best possible quality, as that would be a wasteful and uneconomic policy to follow blindly. The service or product, whether provided internally within the organisation or supplied by an external source, needs to match the user's expectations in terms of accuracy, durability, serviceability and ease of operation. It is obvious from this that the user who will be commissioning the supply must first define the requirements and expectations; then, based on this definition, the user will require specialists, suppliers, contractors or other departments to conform.

11.3 Examples

Outsourced services

The control of quality from outsourced service providers is essential; industrial and office cleaning is a prime example. All premises require cleaning and in all but the smallest the trend is to use specialist contractors who have access to the premises outside normal working hours, either early in the morning or after the close of business. Whenever inviting tenders for such services or placing contracts the facilities manager needs to define a series of conditions as part of the contract that establishes beyond doubt the methods to be followed by the contractor.

These conditions will include a specification of the cleaning operation describing special processes, like anti-static treatment to VDU screens together with the frequency of clean.

Heavily trafficked areas, such as reception, entrances, toilets and catering points will need more intense attention to counteract heavy use and maintain health and safety requirements than will be required for general office areas with less than constant use.

The use of CAFM drawings of the premises with the frequency data applied to each room, backed-up with a written specification at tender stage, avoids disputes over invoices during the contract and makes revisions to the contract simpler to identify and cost whenever the cleaning frequency is revised through use changes.

The drawing extract in Figure 11.1 shows an example of a room with the cleaning frequency highlighted for use by the contractor's operatives. In this example a specification that meets the user's daily quality requirements is established with a full clean weekly and a machine scrub every six months.

All services need to be monitored for quality by the facilities manager or his supervisor and any shortcomings identified. The essence of a successful quality management system is to recognise the existence of shortcomings and implement corrective action. In our cleaning example the problem could be with the operatives, it might result from heavier use or arise from an inadequate initial specification. Whatever the cause,

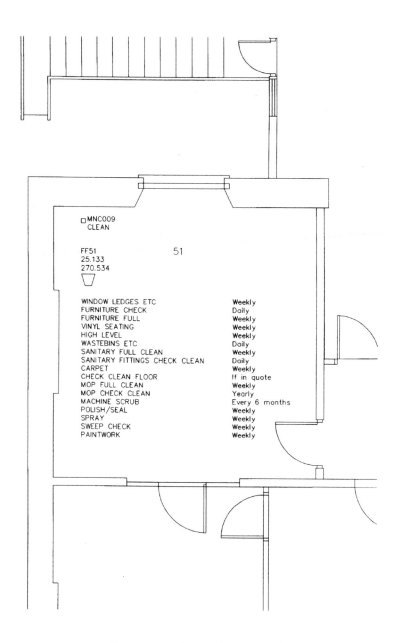

Figure 11.1   Cleaning frequency plan

the service must be raised to provide the correct quality to meet the client's requirements.

Whenever third parties are granted free out-of-hours access to premises a security factor arises that must be considered. Those premises with sophisticated security systems can limit the risk of theft or breaches of data confidentiality, but the facilities manager must make a quality assessment of the operations and devise safeguards. The vetting of references for the proposed cleaners, that is both the contractor and operatives, is an obvious step; less obvious are the internal measures that keep items of value and confidential data secure from abuse. Each situation will be unique and a Quality Assurance System is the ideal vehicle to set out the objectives, analyse the scope of the problem and record the procedures to be followed. Once this is in the system, compliance by all affected individuals is monitored through regular internal quality audits.

Products and consumables

Quality Assurance Systems, when properly applied, set the appropriate quality of a product to satisfy the use without the excessive use of material. The required operational life of the product, which can be consumable stores, equipment, tools, in fact anything used in the course of the business activities, will dictate the standard of manufacture. Take for example copying and printing which in a typical company administrative office will cover the range of internal communication through to external sales brochures, annual accounts and promotional literature.

The quality requirement differs across the range where an analysis quickly establishes the function of the printed material. Internal memorandums, sales reports, stock inventories, are primarily intended to inform, so these need to be clear and legible, but do not need to be copied on quality paper; photocopying or computer forms are adequate. Documents whose purpose is to impress externally and advance the business always benefit from better reproduction; desktop publishing, and colour set out on heavier paper then becomes appropriate as the correct quality. The Quality System controls this aspect and it will be the facilities manager's responsibility to co-ordinate and monitor.

The trend in quality is influenced in many sectors by the increase in the use of disposable items. Often, single-use disposable items are demanded for operational reasons, either health in the case of syringes, or economics with air and oil filters. In both these cases the disposable item is of inferior manufacturing and material quality than the re-usable items that they replace, but in use they are of the correct quality and satisfy the user's expectations.

11.4 Contract and procurement options

The contract and procurement options available to the facilities manager are extensive, with a choice of approach in every case, particularly those relating to buildings. The range of building works, for example, is varied, ranging from minor maintenance of a jobbing nature that does not warrant formal contracts, through planned maintenance and building alterations, to the procurement of completely new facilities.

There are standard forms of contract available to cover all but the smallest supplies which can be adapted to suit each contract's specifics. The facilities manager can ignore all standard forms and write his own but such a task is not for the inexperienced. Contracts reside in files unopened until a dispute arises when all parties to the contract set about scrutinising the content, even down to the choice of wording and interpretation. Whenever these situations arise the tried and tested standard forms that are recognised by the legal profession and are often supported by previous case law provide a more certain assessment of liabilities and therefore should achieve a more rapid settlement.

Not all one-off, specially drafted contracts are a risk but there should be good commercial or operational reasons for their use. In all cases a facilities manager who is not currently experienced in contract drafting is well advised to seek professional assistance. The choice of a consultant from the most appropriate building discipline will save time and money, with professional quantity surveyors, architects and engineers being readily available. The selection of a consultant is best judged by reviewing their relevant experience with projects of a similar nature, then either negotiating or inviting fee tenders from those practices that satisfy on grounds of experience and resources.

If a project is large or complex it may demand too much attention from the facilities manager to administer, causing a conflict with other FM functions. The solution is to place the day-to-day management of the project with a project manager. The project manager can be an employee or a retained consultant and again all the building professional disciplines offer project management services. The facilities manager will initially need to define the principal requirements of the project. Is cost control and value for money the major consideration? Is it the architectural merit of the building or is the building style of little significance? Perhaps the process to be carried out within the building is the all important factor. In each of these cases the discipline of the project manager will lean towards different professions – quantity surveying, architecture or process engineering.

11.5 Organisation and methods

O&M studies have evolved from early applications by the Civil Service into commerce and industry where through evolution other titles have gained common usage like office management systems and procedures and system management. The interest here for the facilities manager is in matching the physical configuration of the buildings to the current thinking on operating methods within the organisation. Changing products, progress, modernisation and fluctuating demand influence operating methods, thus creating a moving target.

The first action in reviewing an O&M study is for the facilities manager to categorise the procedures into important and urgent. These categories are not the same and it is easy for the urgent group to assume an overriding priority in excess of their importance. The successful manager will devote enough effort to the urgent items but channel resources into those important issues which may not be immediately pressing but have significant future implications.

Imagine the situation of two items awaiting the manager's attention; the first is a report that the main computer network is experiencing random unexplained failures, and has been shut down, with operations continuing at reduced efficiency on local networks. The second item is a request from the company board for an assessment of the benefit of outsourcing cleaning, catering and security services.

The initial reaction is to set aside the board request on the grounds that computer network failures take priority over all other matters. In this case operations are continuing and the failure is an inconvenience; so the facilities manager should assess the problem, then brief an assistant or consultant to research the network problem, find the fault and recommend the appropriate corrective action. Having dealt with the initial action, the facilities manager applies his skill to the outsourcing problem, which has far-reaching implications for the staffing, overheads and future competitiveness of the business.

Within existing organisations it is usual to inherit systems and procedures set up by predecessors; these must be reviewed on the basis of why are they needed, their effectiveness and whether better performance criteria should be used to measure that effectiveness.

Whenever a system is monitored it is essential to measure effectiveness in the following areas:

- Level of use.
- User satisfaction.
- Measure of achieved benefit against target.
- Cost of operation.

11.6 Logistics

The study and control of logistics is gaining in status within commercial organisations as they strive to balance the conflicts of minimum resources, raw materials and completed stock on one hand with improved customer service on the other.

The increase in commercial and trade competition as a means of survival in recessionary times has forced all companies to look critically at overhead and direct costs. The major areas of cost are resources employed by the company – both people and equipment, together with cash or credit tied up in materials or warehoused product. The skill of maintaining peak efficiency with efficient supply and distribution lines is well known to military commanders as the study of logistics, but its application to industry is no different in principle if you believe in free trade where companies are battling with their competitors, each seeking an advantage which in business usually means a competitive price or delivery edge.

This, like facilities management of premises, is a make or break activity for companies whereby successful introduction of logistics control and planning more than repays the investment. It is probably not generally practical to combine FM and logistics but the requirements, O&M studies and demands on the facilities raised by logistics planning become a major source of data for the facilities manager to use in adapting the premises to the operations housed within them. The planning element holds the key to success, as the reaction time for logistics decisions to become effective is much shorter than the facilities' reaction time. The closer these can be matched, the greater the commercial benefit.

A downturn in sales is seen as a trend which will prompt the logistics manager to reduce raw material orders, adjust production schedules and de-stock. Adaptation of the premises could include the disposal of temporary or overflow warehousing to maximise the cost savings. Overflow warehousing may be easily vacated but the problem arises when sales recover and the de-stocking is reversed; it may not be possible to reinstate the warehousing if the market has picked up generally and no suitable property is available. The payment of premium rentals to overcome this problem will negate the earlier advantage.

Planning and sound judgement based on accurate logistics data is the key, as there are no thanks for a facilities manager who cannot provide the necessary premises and who stifles recovery or expansion.

11.7   Disaster recovery

What is a disaster? There are the obvious examples of terrorist bombs, storms, floods and earthquakes, but the scope is much wider. Every business, company or organisation has its vulnerable points and anything that disturbs these points will place the entire undertaking at risk.

Many companies are now totally dependent on computer networks for business records, cost and stock control, financial management and communications; loss of these systems, where manual back-up records are no longer available or practical, would be a disaster indeed. Loss of premises, loss of essential energy and interruption of critical material supplies are all potentially catastrophic.

Careful planning and anticipation will greatly reduce the probability of such events occurring but can never completely eliminate the risk, and it is the function of the disaster recovery programme to minimise the effect to the point where the overall undertaking is not placed in jeopardy.

The role of the facilities manager is to seek advice from all departments of the organisation and coordinate an appraisal of the strategic issues. Identify those events that pose a real threat to the organisation and plan in advance the measures that are both practical and available to contain the effects of the events should they occur. It is useful when planning to attempt to assess the probability and therefore the like-lihood of an event in terms of years between occurrences. This data is already available as a prediction in the case of flooding through tides, storms and rivers in spate. These statistics are based on historical data and research into the incidence of previous events will provide an initial pattern for the study.

Once the events are identified, the facilities manager must devise a plan to counter the effects. The plan may range from simple duplication of an essential piece of plant, with changeover procedures predefined and rehearsed, to complex procedures requiring temporary accommo-dation and off-site back-up facilities and records.

An ingeneous facilities manager who is able to coordinate advice from specialists within the organisation and, on particular technical issues, from external experts, will be able to anticipate the disaster event. If properly researched, drawn up and practised, disaster recovery plans will deliver real benefits by eliminating the element of surprise.

Insurance cover should not be overlooked. Many standard business items such as computers, printers and furniture are off-the-shelf pro-ducts, so it is essential to have the correct level of cover to ensure that a claim is valid and will secure prompt payment. There is nothing more distressing than seeing a business fail, following an anticipated event, as a direct result of insurance disputes with loss adjusters.

Case studies

Consider a simple example of an office heated by a conventional circulating hot water system from a central boiler to radiators through-out the building and the consequences of the circulating pump failing during cold weather. When the temperature drops below the comfort level, and certainly when it falls to the legal minimum, there is no alternative but to close the building and send the staff home on full pay until repairs are effected. It is easy to plumb in a parallel standby pump that is isolated by stop valves. Failure of the principal pump is no longer critical to the heating system, as circulation can immediately be switched to the standby pump. The faulty pump can be removed and replaced or repaired and an operational disaster is avoided.

The failure of plant or equipment is the most common cause of disaster and complex issues arise when dealing with process plant, especially if the failure not only shuts down production but creates a health hazard or an environmental risk. Many industrial processes produce toxic fumes as a by-product, and with strict modern pollution controls failure of any plant designed to control the emissions may not directly affect production but will rapidly invite a enforcement order closing the factory. The disruptive effect of such an order, plus the added threat of prosecution and fines, could close the business. The dilemma in this case is to balance of the cost of duplicating plant, which often involves a heavy capital outlay against the probability of a breakdown. The simple solution used in the central heating example is not a viable option in this case, so the facilities manager's task is not to avoid the shutdown but to minimise its effect. Regular planned preventive maintenance is the first line of defence in reducing the incidence of breakdown and striving for a zero-tolerance performance. The issues governing preventive maintenance are covered in chapter 4.

Assuming that a breakdown will occur at some time, emergency call-out procedures with a precontracted specialist maintenance contractor will set the maximum response time for repairs and, based on this period of shutdown, the facilities manager will be able to verify that the cost of accepting some lost production is the most economically viable recovery option.

11.8   Conclusion

The future for successful facilities management must be one of encouraging greater awareness in all organisations that occupy premises. In the field of building and related FM there is encouraging recognition by some professional institutions and many universities of the future demand for trained and qualified managers.

Facilities management has been seen, by the better informed, as the Cinderella of property professionals, both in industry and in the professions. There still is a risk that it could follow the same path as project management where a lack of suitable study courses and qualifications turned project management into a free for all, with no independent control over those who professed to be skilled in the subject. Project management is recovering from this position with increased professionalism and a choice of representative bodies that is being driven by clients who increasingly demand evidence that the manager running their projects is qualified to do so, either through examination or a demonstrable track record.

Facilities management shows several parallels, as the skill here is also a personal and not corporate one; it is the individual's personality and ability that creates success.

As the introduction in chapter 1 stated, buildings and the land that they occupy are finite resources, and extracting the maximum value from them throughout an economic life is just as important as managing declining energy sources.

12 Health and Safety

12.1 The regulations

Health and Safety has been the responsibility of owners and occupiers of buildings for a very long time, but now the regulations are becoming increasingly onerous with both corporate and personal penalties for breach of the regulations reaching significant proportions. It is often thought that individuals in the workplace are largely responsible for their own safety, but the defence of liability of the individual for their actions is far from conclusive; there is a responsibility on the employer to take adequate measures to prevent accidents and injury. The logic behind Health and Safety legislation is to prevent accidents and so the prime responsibility lies with those who create the risk or allow it to continue.

There are two distinct categories of risk for an employer to consider; the first is where the health and safety of employees is concerned while they are at work; the second is the risk to persons not in his employment but arising from the employer's activities, for example, a man working from a ladder where scaffolding should be used. If he falls there is a liability on his employer and a fundamental breach of the regulations for not ensuring proper working practices. If, when the man falls, he lands on a passer-by, then the second category of breach of the regulations has occurred. The employer is again liable. This probably sounds like activities falling within the company's safety officer's remit and little to do with the facilities manager, but unfortunately for the facilities manager the legislation is written in terms that spreads the personal liability for corporate failures in a wide net.

The facilities manager has a direct responsibility for maintenance, equipment, activity flow of premises and the general occupancy standards, all of which have to satisfy health and safety requirements.

12.2 Risk assessment

The regulations that came into force in January 1993 now require the employer to carry out a suitable and sufficient assessment of health and safety risks to employees and others, with the intention of identifying the actions or measures needed to comply with the statutory requirements.

This all sounds somewhat draconian, but past experience has demonstrated the need to enforce safety measures as many employers and employees are unaware of good practice or believe that compliance restricts their productivity and therefore earnings. There is, however, an excellent case for measures that reduce the incidence of accidents and health problems; the humanitarian context is obvious in that nobody wishes to encounter avoidable suffering and the economic considerations are enormous.

Lost production time runs to tens of millions of man/days per annum in the UK costing up to £5 billion and then there is the insurance aspect with claims running close to £1 billion. The insurance aspect carries two further considerations; first there is the extraordinary waste of court and litigation resources in reaching often contentious settlements and the basic principle of insurance that all claims settled need to be taken into account and recovered through future premiums. There is also the growing problems of shortage of underwriting capacity in the insurance markets that could render some activities uninsurable.

The problem with encouraging health and safety response to risk assessment on the economic argument is that it is impossible to evaluate the saving to an employer of introducing safety measures just on the arbitrary basis of assuming the number and severity of incidents avoided.

The requirement to undertake risk assessments applies to every employment, including the self-employed, and where there are more than five employees the assessments must be properly recorded.

It is clear that the application of the regulations could be taken to extremes, so an element of judgement is permitted whereby insignificant risks that are not compounded by the employer's activities may be ignored. This is an area where the combined skill of the facilities manager and the safety officer should be used to define those items of equipment or work activities that fall outside the regulations, leaving a definitive register of the remainder that require assessment. The risk assessment of equipment and machines in the working environment has already been described in chapter 6 in relation to asset registers.

The purpose is to avoid the risk completely by going to the core of the activity and devising safety measures or revised procedures that use the best current technology and recognise the specific requirements of the individual employees engaged on assessed activities. Office furniture, workbenches and other working areas that adjust for height will encourage shared use by individuals of varying stature. A more comfortable working environment greatly reduces fatigue and therefore the chance of accidents.

Always ensure that everyone understands the safety requirements for their activities. Assessments are active procedures, not just notices that through familiarity become ignored; also active procedures are living directives that need to change through time to maintain currency with technology and working methods.

The regulations demand that an employer nominates one or more persons to assist in the assessment and those persons must be competent. The test of competence in this context must have due regard to the process or equipment being assessed; it is clear that an individual with practical working experience of the equipment will be better qualified to identify and even anticipate risk than one who must rely on theoretical evaluation.

It is therefore the case that several nominated persons may be required in a complex working environment and it is prudent to record each nominee's qualifications and experience, together with an unambiguous defined scope of the areas they will be assisting on the risk assessment.

As the facilities manager you will not be expected to become an expert in safety but you will be the best equipped to record the definitive list of assessments, log the nominated individual's identities against the assessments and ensure that a periodically managed review is undertaken.

The review of assessments is important to ensure that they remain current and take account of changing working practices. The use of equipment changes through time as a result of varying workloads, different personnel or operatives and technical advances. Research into health implications and improved knowledge of hazardous substances is an external factor with great significance to the employer. The problems associated with asbestos for example are well-known now, but there was a time when it was considered to be a safe, efficient industrial material. It is prudent to assume that there are substances and processes in uncontrolled use today that will become recognised as dangerous in the future.

The most effective way of controlling assessment reviews is to impose a programme that requires a formally recorded audit of the current risk assessment at predetermined intervals. This is a procedure successfully adopted in quality assurance systems and in terms of any company's quality system is a requirement in compliance with ISO 9000.

The frequency of reviews needs to be determined in advance and should be not less than annually.

The review may be complex where fundamental changes are necessary or just a positive record that the current assessment remains valid. In all cases the undertaking of a review needs to be recorded and this, together with all the other data covering nominated persons and the like, is readily stored by the asset register database in the case of equipment or in a separate activity database covering processes.

Small companies may find it difficult to identify a suitable nominee from within their own staff to undertake assessments, so the use of an outside consultant will be an appropriate solution. This has the benefit of economy where the assistance required is intermittent. Outside consultants are most successfully employed whenever a specific expertise is needed and this would apply to companies of all sizes.

The use of an outside consultant poses some problems and does not allow an employer to avoid his responsibilities under the legislation. Any such consultant will not be as familiar with the company's overall operations, responsibilities and personnel as would an individual from within, so in order to carry out assessments he must be made aware of all factors affecting his task. Consultants will need to be fully informed of the current health and safety directives operated by the company and be allowed reasonably free access to company personnel and safety records. Any failure to brief the consultant fully on these factors could make his assessments inadequate and place the company, its employees responsible for safety and directors at risk from prosecution for non-compliance with the regulations or, in the worst case, liable in a damages action following a safety incident.

So far the facilities manager's role in health and safety has been to support other experts with data, but employers are required to deal with dangers and danger areas. Procedures are required that are activated whenever an event of serious and imminent danger to persons at work occurs. The most obvious of these involve evacuation of the workplace and will entail the use of safety equipment. Items like the obvious fire-fighting installations will be logged on a facilities management database that ensures they are serviced and checked and, so long as this servicing has been adequately devised and carried out, these items may be expected to function properly.

The risks that the facilities manager must anticipate are also less obvious in that in an emergency set escape routes are to be followed and, because panic is a factor, evacuees, however well rehearsed, can become disorientated. Automatic closing of fire doors/shutters actively contains danger; similarly, physically preventing access to danger areas reduces the risk of injury. All equipment activating shutters, doors and the like need to be in good working order and regularly checked for improper use. Hot weather and uncomfortable working conditions have often encouraged fire doors to be wedged open, ironically often with a fire extinguisher removed from its logged location.

Restricted access in the workplace applies at times other than emergencies, especially if activities hazardous to untrained or unprotected staff are involved. Radiography in hospital premises presents a hazard to unauthorised personnel and active use requires door and screens to be in place and a proper means of warning or prevention to restrict access while in use.

In some cases the use of warning notices or 'no entry' red lights will be an adequate safeguard; in high-risk situations a physical bar will be necessary. The assessment of measures required and their design is not the particular skill of the facilities manager, but their proper operation is.

One of the simplest methods of controlling access to authorised personnel is of course locked doors; even key suiting to compel predetermined access routes is straightforward by only allowing the keyholder to open the doors necessary to follow his permitted access route, all other door locks being inoperable by his key.

The facilities manager controls the suiting, logs the issue of keys and retains all this data on the CAFM system. Each door in the chain is labelled with an attribute that within the database shows is compatible suiting and now, with the introduction of reliable and relatively inexpensive programmable locks, access routes and access restrictions may be devised and modified without the delay of lock and key changing associated with traditional locks. This ability has benefits beyond health and safety into security, even to restricting access within programmable time/date zones.

The latest regulations have increased the employee's responsibilities in respect of risk assessment in that each employee now has a statutory obligation to inform the safety nominee of any working circumstances that will affect the safety of any persons and to tell the employer of any shortcomings in the safety procedures. This can only become effective once the employees have been adequately trained.

12.3 Health and safety policy

The provision of a company health and safety policy is essential to cover the requirements of properly recorded risk assessments and, as far as the facilities manager is concerned, needs to address the organisation of the workplace activities.

The facilities manager will log and control the proper maintenance and testing of workplace equipment. If the company's activities extend beyond the permanent workplace, then it will again be the facilities manager's responsibility to log any equipment taken to the remote location. The safe and proper use of the equipment is the nominated safety officer's responsibility, but on the basis that employees are now required to report potential risks these need to be recorded by the facilities manager whenever the risk is caused by the malfunction of any logged equipment.

The health and safety policy must be freely available to all personnel, be properly understood and, where specific, be covered by training.

12.4 Manual handling operations

The regulations define manual handling operations as any transporting or supporting of a load (including the lifting, putting down, pushing, pulling, carrying or moving) by hand or by bodily force.

As with risk assessment it is necessary for the employer to identify any hazards, take steps to avoid them and, if that is not possible, document the hazard with a view to reducing the risk as far as is reasonably possible. The problem this presents to the employer is the definition of reasonableness; it is imprecise, open to opinion, varying interpretations and argument, particularly if an actionable incident has occurred.

If we accept that the handling of products, goods and the like is fundamental to the core business activities, the facilities manager's contribution to risk elimination or at least reduction is in the configuration of the workplace. Automation that dispenses with manual handling eliminates this risk, but is seldom possible, so reference to Regulation 4(1)(b)(i) in Schedule 1 suggests a structured approach to the assessment under the headings of:

- The task.
- The load.
- The working environment.
- Individual capacity.

The facilities manager's contribution is in the third category of working environment. Each activity will be different so will require specific attention and the facilities manager's practical approach to satisfying production requirements without imposing an excessively rigid working environment is invaluable. This is best illustrated by examples, but a walk round most industrial premises, many office and non-industrial establishments will identify any handling requirements with some degree of injury risk.

Loading and unloading through goods receipt and dispatch areas are the obvious ones; often as there is a temptation to handle excessive loads. Dock levellers are commonplace and need to be capable of adjusting to the full range of vehicles in use but once the goods are off the vehicle and into the building how are they handled? Are the goods paletted or loose, are conveyors needed or can handling and distribution be automated by pumping or gravity feed?

In many of these instances the facilities manager has a direct interest in the space planning exercise that creates an efficient work flow; he is interested in the fixed and mobile handling equipment in terms of maintenance and reliability.

Stacking, racking and storage of both incoming components or materials and the planned flow through the manufacturing process to the point of dispatch of the finished product is a space and activity flow exercise, and the means of handling has a direct bearing on the solution. It is possible that a mechanical handling routine can become significantly economic if the cheapest solution is ruled out on manual handling grounds. It is an objective comparison on cost–benefit grounds where the facilities manager can draw on and balance conflicting priorities of production efficiency against the greater capital cost of mechanical handling plant.

A change from manual to mechanical handling of goods, materials or finished products depends on a number of factors, including movement, volume, premises layout and speed of response. The first two considerations are obvious in that small volume movement will not justify the cost of mechanical handling and the premises must suit whatever mechanical systems are proposed. The systems fall into categories using conveyors, fork lifts, automated picking and gravity systems.

Some high volume turnover industries could not exist without mechanical handling. In manufacturing, the motor industry is an excellent example where progress has developed the process from highly labour-intensive between the two world wars to the latest automated production lines that seek to reduce the human involvement. The retail industry, especially the food superstore sector, handles stock very efficiently with small stock rooms supplied by radio-directed road haulage from centralised distribution depots. This is the 'just-in-time' principle that seeks to carry the minimum of stock in each store but respond to restocking demands almost instantly to prevent stock on the sales floor running out. The cost of such sophisticated handling and distribution systems is covered by the reduced capital investment in warehouse stock. In fact it is the aim to use the retailer's credit arrangements with produce suppliers to minimize the retailer's stock holding burden and achieve the store customer's cash in the checkout till before the supplier's invoice is settled. This is the ultimate in positive cashflow that would be impossible without computerised stock control and highly developed distribution.

Gravity distribution, usually of raw materials, is almost a free service. Once the initial capital cost of arranging for supplies to be made at high level the materials may be distributed on demand throughout the workplace. Liquids, granular materials and material chips can be handled in this way, occasionally assisted by compressed air. Success in this approach needs adequate design of the premises as these systems can become inflexible if supply routes become too long and, if there is a health hazard intrinsic in the material, proper controls are essential to contain leakage and spills. The dairy industry uses gravity feed extensively as does the food industry in grain handling and in plastic bottle manufacturing, where plastic chips are silo-stored before distribution to the blowing plant.

12.5 Display screen and associated equipment

This covers any alphanumeric or graphic display screen irrespective of the use involved. This has wide-ranging applications from word processing, through computers, design systems to VDU monitors in process control. It is not restricted to particular areas of the workplace; it applies to offices, design departments, research and production.

With the display screen comes a user/operator which is somebody who uses the display as a significant part of their normal working activities. There is no distinction between employment status other than users are employees and operators are self-employed. The display screen will be linked to other equipment comprising a work station including computer/processor, disk drives, printers, modems, phone, desk and seating.

The facilities manager will log all the individual items of equipment brought together to create work stations for specific purposes in his CAFM Asset Register.

As it is the employer's responsibility to analyse the risk of fatigue (principally visual), together with mental stress associated with each work station, this assessment needs to:

- Be co-ordinated in approach.
- Geared to the level of risk.
- Cover all aspects of use.
- Draw information from employer and user/operator.

The ideal ergonomics of the work station will be established by the health and safety officer, and the facilities manager then strives to achieve the siting and orientation of the work station with the workspace that achieves the environment closest to the ideal. This is an exercise in space planning, activity layout, lighting, heating/cooling and sound attenuation. Taking these considerations in turn the work station needs to be sited where best to satisfy the receipt/processing of data and be available to the user/operator. In the case of word processing or accounts processing the user/operator and the work station are a unit that can be placed at will within the offices, whereas the siting of a work station monitoring production will be dictated by the production process. The use of a CAFM system allows alternative solutions to be trial tested in advance of installation – a worthwhile exercise whenever data cabling and networks are being planned. Activity analysis will show good working layouts for work stations dictated by departmental or individual interfaces, the needs to network and data exchange.

Lighting, heating, cooling and sound attenuation are all workspace environmental considerations which the facilities manager must take into account. Strong natural light can be a problem with VDUs, causing visual fatigue; conversely, an isolated working area and no direct contact with the world outside is a source of mental stress in users/operators. The answer is usually shading to control strong natural light with purpose-designed artificial light to eliminate glare. The control of an acceptable working temperature throughout all the seasons is a universal goal in the workplace, but an added burden arises from heat generated from concentrations of business machines. The facilities manager with the M&E engineer needs to consider heat dissipation and balance areas with high equipment heat gain and building aspect; in other words, do not site departments with high equipment loadings on the elevations suffering the greatest solar gain, or your company will finish up with unhappy staff and larger than necessary bills for comfort cooling.

Noise is often overlooked and some electronic equipment generates high and intrusive noise levels; printers, especially high-speed models, are distracting and subconsciously exhausting. Acoustic hoods solve isolated problems and detached print rooms linked by the network remove the distraction from the users/operators' immediate environment.

12.6 Work equipment

All work equipment provided by employers must be suitable and properly maintained and, where equipment is shared by a number of operatives, the health and safety responsibility rests with the prime operator. Equipment provided by employees and sanctioned by the employer becomes the employer's responsibility.

There are two major points here; first, if a company provides equipment and allows it to be used by others the company is responsible for its safe performance; second, it is not good enough just to log company-provided equipment on the health and safety database if employees provide their own.

The regulations require every employer to ensure that work equipment is so constructed or adapted as to be suitable for the purpose for which it is used or provided. This sounds all very logical but, bearing in mind that the employer is responsible for the employee's use of the equipment, how does the employer legislate against inappropriate use that gives rise to an infringement of the regulations?

Whenever the use of equipment could give rise to such a problem it should already have been recognised and be covered by a risk assessment. The risk assessment in itself is of little value unless operating limits

and procedures are devised, recorded and made available to the operatives and the operatives are trained in the proper use.

The risk assessment, operating limits, procedures and training fall to
the safety officer but the facilities manager logs them through the asset
register or activity database. In this way any incident causing an injury
can be quickly cross-related to any similar working procedures and
corrective action applied to reduce risk generally.

The use of hydraulic lifting equipment during maintenance operations that causes damage to the component being lifted through insufficient load spreading would be a typical example for a corrective action
to all similar operating procedures.

The choice of work equipment rests with the employer and the
facilities manager can help the decision-making process through cost–
benefit analysis of the alternatives. But before this consideration the
regulations require the employer to assess the risk to health and safety
and ensure that all equipment acquired meets the criteria.

The regulations require equipment to be maintained and records of
planned maintenance together with historical evidence of compliance
with the maintenance plan must be kept for inspection. This record can
be kept by the facilities manager as part of the asset register and
whenever an operation carries greater risks or needs particular training
to undertake, the use of nominated persons for such operations is
logged to the register.

Breach of the Provision and Use of Work Equipment Regulations gives
rise to criminal proceedings that may be brought by the Health and
Safety Executive, and Local Authority civil claims may also follow such a
prosecution.

12.7 Personal protective equipment

The need, or indeed the benefit, of protective equipment will be recognised through the risk assessment process from which will come the
operational directives that make staff and operatives aware of their
obligations. Whenever it is necessary or beneficial to provide protective
equipment this may be logged as a field in the health and safety
database; the extent of the equipment will be dictated by the process
involved.

There is a further consideration, and that is whether the equipment is
maintained at the activity location for shared use by any operative or is

issued to specific individuals and the operation concerned restricted to these named operatives. Either approach has advantages and disadvantages that present differing management tasks for the facilities manager. The shared use situation is flexible from an operational point view but suffers from a low responsibility tag whereby it is difficult to ensure that the equipment is always complete and in good working order. It is human nature to avoid direct responsibility, particularly when damage or loss occurs and the facilities manager cannot rely on such problems being spontaneously reported. The specific issues of equipment overcomes the responsibility factor but restricts operational flexibility.

The choice will be dictated in most cases by the activity and often by the skill level required by the activity. There are many examples but picking one here helps to illustrate the point. The chemical industry has a higher than average incidence of risk activities requiring special procedures and protective equipment. Equipment includes helmets and eye protection through to safety suits and breathing apparatus. The processes requiring helmets and eye protection may be less specialised and therefore the equipment is made available at the activity location on a need-to-use basis. Safety suits and breathing apparatus imply higher skill levels, higher risks and therefore trained named individuals. If the risks of personal injury are higher in the latter cases, then concentrating the responsibility for personal protective equipment with that individual greatly benefits the risk analysis.

The facilities manager's task will be to log the issue of personal protective equipment as directed by the safety officer, set up an internal audit procedure to verify that all the protective equipment logged on the asset register is in place and check at predetermined intervals that it is all in full working order.

An additional responsibility is the provision and proper use of storage for personal protective equipment and here the facilities manager must establish the specific storage requirements and arrange suitable provisions.

12.8 The Construction (Design and Management) Regulations 1994

These regulations came into force in March 1995 with the express objective of improving the accident and safety record of the construction industry. Their impact extends beyond the design and construction stages of projects in that for the first time there are now regulations requiring the client, designers and contractors to consider not just construction hazards, but also hazards that may affect the occupiers and users of the completed building.

It is mandatory to prepare a preconstruction Health and Safety Plan during the design stage of projects, and this is the responsibility of the Planning Supervisor. There are two mandatory appointments that a client must now make on every qualifying project; a Planning Supervisor and the Principal Contractor. The Planning Supervisor must be suitably qualified, experienced and resourced to carry out his obligations, as defined in regulation 14. These responsibilities include ensuring as far as is practicable that the designers of the project properly consider the safety aspects of their designs, with the overriding proviso that not all risks can be designed out so those that remain must be controlled. The Planning Supervisor is very much the front-end adviser and is responsible for preparing the Health and Safety Plan for the project. This should identify the known hazards on the site, those arising from adjoining land uses and those remaining in the design that can not be designed out. The Principal Contractor is not necessarily the main contractor, but again the appointee must demonstrate the necessary competence and resources to fulfil the obligations. The Principal Contractor is primarily responsible for developing the Planning Supervisor's preconstruction Health and Safety Plan into a plan that controls safety throughout the on-site construction stage. Responsibility for health and safety matters is transferred from the Planning Supervisor to the Principal Contractor upon commencement of the construction work, although the Planning Supervisor retains the task of coordinating the designers' risk assessment for any design development that occurs during the construction phase.

The Planning Supervisor is also responsible for collecting all the project's health and safety information at the end of the construction period and compiling the Health and Safety File, which must contain all relevant information on occupational hazards and safe operating procedures that apply to the building following occupation. This file is a mandatory document that the client must retain for as long as an interest is maintained in the building. If that interest is disposed of, the client is obliged to pass on the file to the new owner.

Although this is not intended to be a definitive guide to the regulations, it is necessary to point out that any facilities manager reviewing construction work or the installation of process plant and equipment needs to establish whether the project falls within the scope of the regulations and if so to appoint a Planning Supervisor at the earliest opportunity. Regulation 3 sets out the qualifying criteria for applicable projects as follows:

- Those with more than four persons working on the site.
- The work will exceed 30 days.
- Demolitions are part of the work.

Work on houses for owner-occupier domestic clients lies outside the regulations, but houses owned by housing associations and letting organisations fall within their scope.

There is a further obligation to notify projects to the Health and Safety Executive on a standard form entitled 'Notification of a project' and referenced as form 'F10' – this responsibility rests with the Planning Supervisor.

Failure to comply with the regulations can lead to prosecution under criminal law.

The Planning Supervisor will lead the facilities manager through the requirements, but there are several useful publications by the Health and Safety Executive that are valuable reference material for those facilities managers who wish to study the responsibilities in more detail. The leading document is *Managing construction for health and safety Construction (Design and Management) Regulations 1994*, supported by *Designing for health and safety in construction*, *A guide to managing health and safety in construction* and *Health and Safety in Construction*.

Several references have been made to the regulations throughout this book and the following sections elaborate on these references.

12.9 The health and safety file

This document, which is retained throughout the lifetime of the building, should contain all information that will assist any person carrying out further work on the structure at any time. It is a living document that needs to be updated as further work is done on the building in order to keep the information current. As a rule the file will contain:

- 'As built' record drawings.
- Details of the construction.
- Information on installed equipment.
- Maintenance requirements.

- Manuals and certificates provided by specialist contractors and suppliers.
- Information on the location of utilities and services.

When correctly assembled, the file is a very valuable point of reference for facilities managers and is effectively a log book.

The file must be held in a secure place and be available for reference purposes to any person who needs access to the information it contains. The responsibility placed on the building owner/occupier to hold the file securely can conflict with the need for it to be readily available for reference, so in complex buildings it is sensible, for example, not to treat the O & M manuals as part of the file. An unambiguous reference to the manuals and where they are kept is sufficient.

12.10 Designers' and principal contractor's responsibilities

Designers are now required to design with safety in mind and are expressly charged with the task of identifying construction and occupational risks arising from the building. They must follow a procedure set out in the regulations to minimise the impact of the foreseeable risks in the following order of priority:

- Design to avoid all foreseeable risks.
- Combat risks at source to any person carrying out construction, cleaning or at work in the building.
- Give priority to measures that protect the maximum number of persons.

The last of these points accepts that risks cannot be totally eliminated and as such designers are now responsible for researching the option that places the least number of persons at risk. A typical instance would be installing additional guard rails on an exposed roof. Here the construction workers installing the rails face an added risk, but this is outweighed by the long-term benefits provided by the rails to maintenance operatives throughout the life of the building. Remember that it is often more effective to control a construction risk with the cooperation of a responsible contractor than to attempt to devise 'idiot proof' safeguards for all the future occupants.

Principal Contractors are responsible for safe working practices during the construction period and for ensuring that all operations are properly planned, have the appropriate resources in plant and labour and that all contractors engaged on the works operate within the safety rules set by the Principal Contractor. The Principal Contractor is also required to co-operate with the Planning Supervisor.

12.11 The client's responsibilities

The client, who may be represented by the facilities manager, has a number of responsibilities under the regulations. Figure 12.1 acts as a checklist of these obligations.

12.12 Conclusions

The interpretation and application of the Health and Safety Regulations is a specialist skill and the purpose of this chapter is not to place the facilities manager automatically in the role of the safety officer. Its purpose is to raise awareness of this legislation and its potential effect on the use of premises on the understanding that health and safety measures under the regulations will take precedence over all other operational considerations and failure to do so incurs both criminal and civil penalties.

As in other aspects of the facilities manager's job a strongly developed practical approach to problem-solving, based on a sound knowledge of buildings, will reach the solution that best satisfies the regulation and production requirements.

As a summary, this chapter has suggested that facilities managers' interest in health and safety covers the following categories:

- Safe and proper functioning of the premises and equipment.
- Logging and interrogating databases – asset registers for risk analyses.
- Flagging up danger areas and operating restricted access measures.
- Control the programme of internal safety audits.
- Achieving the most appropriate allocation of space to particular departments/activities.
- Database controlling issue, storage, testing and maintenance of work equipment and safety equipment.

	Milestone	Client's Duties	Checked
1	As soon as possible, and certainly at the point when the project ceases to be a feasibility study	Appoint a Planning Supervisor (PS) Confirm competency of designers Review designer's briefs for H&S content *Sign off date*	☐ ☐ ☐
2	Throughout the project design stage	Provide H&S information on the site, buildings and project to PS, e.g.: 1. Site/ground conditions. 2. Contamination reports etc. 3. Hazardous materials in existing structures. 4. Statutory notices/prohibition notices. 5. Client's hazardous operations on site. 6. Existing H&S files. 7. As built drawings/schedules etc. *Sign off date*	☐ ☐ ☐ ☐ ☐ ☐ ☐
3	At tender stage	Ensure that H&S responsibilities are placed on the Principal Contractor (PC) and appropriate prelim items are included in the tender documents *Sign off date*	☐
4	As soon as possible in the design stage	Appoint a Principal Contractor (PC) *Sign off date*	☐
5	Prior to appointment	Ensure that those you appoint are competent and adequately resourced to carry out the H&S responsibilities *Sign off date*	☐
6	Before work starts on site	Ensure that the PC has prepared an adequate H&S Plan and that the PS is available to advise on its adequacy *Sign off date*	☐
7	As soon as possible after project completion on site	Ensure that the H&S File is passed to you by the PS *Sign off date*	☐
8	For as long as you retain an interest in the structure	Keep the H&S File in secure document storage and make it readily available to any persons with a legitimate need to consult the file	☐

Figure 12.1   Checklist of client's duties

13 The Property Portfolio

13.1 Introduction

Any organisation's property portfolio is created by acquisition. The components of the estate may be:

- Purchased new or second-hand.
- Developed from scratch.
- Extensions of the existing premises.
- Acquired as a direct result of the acquisition of another company.

No matter which acquisition path is chosen, all present the facilities manager with challenges. The direct acquisition of property is perhaps the most straightforward in that all needs should have been properly defined before the search for premises commenced so the issue to be addressed is the inevitable compromise that will have to be made, as it is unlikely that the perfect building will be found. The option to develop from scratch offers the best opportunity for success in operational terms as there will be no need to accept an earlier owner's or developer's design, but nevertheless the finished article will still be a compromise. The building that perfectly matches the user's needs has yet to be designed.

The final route – acquisition of another company that arrives with its own portfolio of property – is by far the most difficult. Other than as a book valuation of the asset on the company balance sheet, the property is seldom the motive for the acquisition and the facilities manager is then expected to integrate the operational activities of the merged companies and resolve duplication in property. This often comes with the added pressure to realise and maximise funds from surplus assets, including the property, to set against the purchase price paid for the overall acquisition. This rationalisation of the enlarged estate will initially be dictated in principle by the company's board of directors; thereafter the facilities manager's task is to implement these principles. While the facilities manager is the key player in the task, due consultation with other departments in the company will be required to take account of economic priorities, human resource management and production management. The amalgamation of two companies' property portfolios can easily create an estate that is 25 to 30 per cent larger than needed for economic operation of the new enlarged company. The ultimate success of the enterprise will depend on the skill of the facilities manager in disposing of the surplus, in such a way that the retained property fits the board's principles with regard to quality, style and strategic location. In all cases of acquisition that are not primarily for the purpose of asset stripping but are intended to create a stronger trading enterprise, the disposal of property will be spread across both companies with the express purpose of retaining the best. Difficult decisions will have to be taken, as there will undoubtedly be relocations and job losses that will be viewed as a betrayal, particularly those affecting the acquirer.

13.2 Acquisition

Case study

There are two motor dealerships in a town. Rationalisation of the dealer network means that one loses its franchise because of its inability to invest in the manufacturer's new corporate image and install new diagnostic and service equipment. The other dealer retains its franchise and does not wish its competitor's business to be taken over by an outside dealer. The exercise is that of protecting market share in the town and making it less attractive for an outsider, so the successful dealer offers to buy out the other's interests. One main dealer now exists in the town but is burdened with two sets of service facilities, showrooms and offices.

The task of the facilities manager is to review all the property and equipment of the combined dealerships and establish the most efficient and profitable use of the resources. This will highlight the facilities that are surplus to requirement and should therefore be earmarked for disposal. The surplus tools and equipment are portable and can be sold out of the area; the premises are not portable and must be disposed of at source. The problem is that the premises are specific in their purpose and simple disposal by auction is likely to result in their purchase by another motor dealer; which would totally defeat the purpose of the acquisition.

It is therefore essential that, as part of the acquisition process, the rationalisation and true disposal costs of assets are assessed. In this case the book asset value of the property will be seriously reduced if it is sold with restrictions imposed on its future use in order to eliminate the competition factor. Alternatively, significant costs would be incurred prior to disposal if the surplus premises were converted to another use, including both delays and the cost of dealing with planning issues. Property disposal is a specialist activity and the facilities manager is well advised to seek professional help. Planning, building control and fire certificates are all examples of the external regulatory controls that will apply to commercial premises, and failure to address these requirements in advance of the disposal campaign is to run the risk of seriously reducing the price achieved from the disposal. Again the facilities manager should consider professional help as there will be no thanks for underselling an asset.

Rationalisation and disposal costs are often overlooked and can cause serious financial problems for the acquiring company if a book value based on original trading use is relied upon when structuring the purchase price.

Unfortunately, in many cases the facilities manager is not consulted at this wheeling and dealing stage but is expected to work miracles once the deal becomes binding. This is an issue of strategic management set at board level to acquire another company and integrate the trading operations, usually motivated by the desire for increased profits and market share, and on occasion to secure another company's patents and product research. The facilities manager's role as facilitator is to exercise the detailed management necessary to achieve the strategic goals. Successful facilities managers are those who follow the more difficult proactive management approach.

Property acquired to satisfy the need for new premises, for expansion, to accommodate revised production methods or to address a geographical need of the business can present the same disposal problems as the above case study, but in many cases the existing premises will not be vacated and hence will not be available to competitors. Making the premises suitable for the company's operations is the facilities manager's task, in conjunction with other departments, including production management and finance. Buildings purchased from developers, especially if they were completed before the negotiations to purchase or rent commenced, will need to be fitted out to allow the most effective use of the space. A typical developer's building is constructed to conform with the investment criteria set out by the property market and driven by the pressures of supply and demand. Letting agents and disposal surveyors operate to a series of rules that seek to construct a universal building, be it a factory, warehouse or office, that will appeal to the widest possible market at the point of disposal.

Developers often act as facilitators in the development process by assembling ownership of building sites (often from a number of individual ownerships), commissioning designs and then seeking funding from a bank or other institution. The developer's profit comes from the successful sale of the building to the end user, or more commonly by securing a lease from an occupier. The lease becomes an investment through its rental income, and can be held by the developer in a property portfolio or may be sold to an investment institution for a price based on the capitalisation of the rental income over the lifetime of the lease. If the developer has been skilful in creating and marketing the development, the return from the sale will reward him well for the initial risk-taking.

In the latter case of leased premises, if you are the facilities manager of a tenant company you will need to understand the responsibilities and restrictions imposed by the terms of the lease and plan accordingly. Buildings secured on a lease are ultimately controlled by the landlord, and therefore it may not be possible to alter the building significantly. Such buildings are normally constructed to 'developer's shell' specification level and will require fitting out, including carpets, partitions, furniture and services. When planning the fitting out remember that your operations will change in line with market developments during the period of occupation. Demand for your company's services will vary, IT developments will have an impact on how you work and staffing levels could fluctuate. Flexibility that allows the layouts and use of space to be varied easily and economically is the key to success, with the final consideration that if the property is leased you will be required to remove all the fitting out at the end of the lease, returning the building to the original developer's shell state. This can be an expensive cost on top of the significant expense of moving to the next location.

13.3 Refurbishment, alteration or relocation

Should your company decide that the existing premises are no longer adequate and it sets up a study of its future facilities requirements, at once a bewildering range of options appear. Can the future requirements be satisfied by the existing facilities with a programme of refurbishment? Is the problem such that the existing facilities will suffice after refurbishment, alteration perhaps extension? Is the problem more radical, requiring relocation?

There are a number of fundamental questions to ask when reviewing these options, as shown in Figure 13.1. As with all strategy options that affect the overall performance of your company, the simple premises appraisal based on these eleven questions cannot be viewed in isolation. The financial burden of any change must be affordable, so the cost appraisal of any change needs to include the consequential cost of hiring solicitors, accountants and other consultants, together with a realistic estimate of the cost of disruption, including lost production.

The operational implications cannot be ignored, particularly if the familiar working environment is to be changed by replanning, extending or relocating.

As the facilities manager, it is your task to involve the financial and operational sectors of your company and pull together a comprehensive report that presents the business case accurately.

13.4   Case study

A national company owns a 1960s office building on a city centre site. The company wishes to remain at this location but the working environment of the building does not conform to current office standards. The optimum solution is to decant the staff, demolish the building and redevelop the site. The planning authority grants permission for the demolition and redevelopment but places a height restriction on the new building that means the loss of two floors. The scheme is no longer financially viable owing to the reduction in the development plot ratio and the fact that the decanted staff would not all return and fit into the new building. The plot ratio is the ratio of floor space to site size, and the greater the ratio, the higher the investment value of the development.

The planning authority cannot prevent the existing building being retained in its original size so the solution in this case is to strip back the building to its basic structural components and carry out a major refurbishment of the existing structure.

The completed project has resulted in an office that will be viable beyond the millennium and although it is more of a compromise than the new development would have been, the staff have high-quality working space and the investment value to the portfolio is maintained.

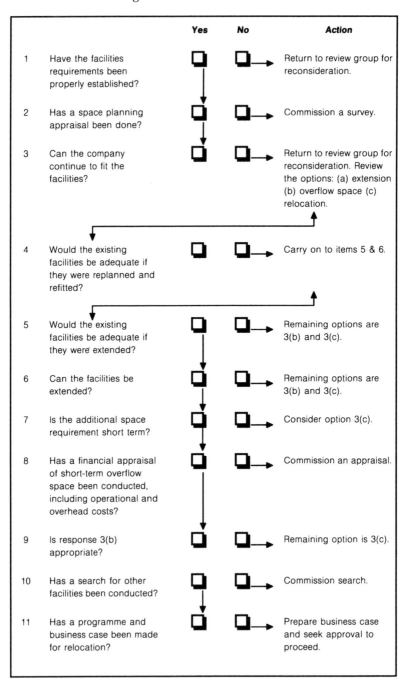

		Yes	No	Action
1	Have the facilities requirements been properly established?	☐	☐ →	Return to review group for reconsideration.
2	Has a space planning appraisal been done?	☐	☐ →	Commission a survey.
3	Can the company continue to fit the facilities?	☐	☐ →	Return to review group for reconsideration. Review the options: (a) extension (b) overflow space (c) relocation.
4	Would the existing facilities be adequate if they were replanned and refitted?	☐	☐ →	Carry on to items 5 & 6.
5	Would the existing facilities be adequate if they were extended?	☐	☐ →	Remaining options are 3(b) and 3(c).
6	Can the facilities be extended?	☐	☐ →	Remaining options are 3(b) and 3(c).
7	Is the additional space requirement short term?	☐	☐ →	Consider option 3(c).
8	Has a financial appraisal of short-term overflow space been conducted, including operational and overhead costs?	☐	☐ →	Commission an appraisal.
9	Is response 3(b) appropriate?	☐	☐ →	Remaining option is 3(c).
10	Has a search for other facilities been conducted?	☐	☐ →	Commission search.
11	Has a programme and business case been made for relocation?	☐	☐ →	Prepare business case and seek approval to proceed.

Figure 13.1   Refurbishment, alteration or relocation flow diagram

13.5 Managing the portfolio

Any business with a portfolio of property, be it a single building or a campus, all in one location or spread geographically, rented or owned freehold, needs to manage this asset to prevent it from becoming an overbearing burden on overheads.

Every property portfolio contains risks and the facilities manager, when tasked with the property function, needs to have log book information on all the premises. This log book should contain details of the following for each building:

- Age and use.
- Leasehold or freehold.
- Life remaining within the portfolio.
- The Health and Safety File under the 1994 CDM Regulations
- Known hazards.
- O & M manuals.

The Health and Safety file is a mandatory document for all qualifying buildings and the requirements are detailed in chapter 12. The other records listed above, while not mandatory, are essential for the efficient operation of the facilities. Other chapters detail techniques for logging and controlling maintenance, asset registers, space planning and risk analysis of known hazards.

Age and use is an obvious issue, as older and more dilapidated property poses a greater risk of high maintenance costs and will probably present the most difficulties when it comes to disposal. An existing portfolio can only be managed to minimise this risk. In the case of acquisition by any means, new property on the portfolio needs to have all risks analysed as part of the viability study.

Many companies cannot afford to own the freehold of their premises and many others could choose to retain their capital to support their core business. As a result the norm is to lease property. Even when a company commissions and develops a new building for its own use, this is often done on a sale and leaseback arrangement. Under this arrangement the company raises the funds for site acquisition and development out of capital or a short-term development loan, then sells the development as an investment to a financial institution or property company. The institution becomes the landlord and enters into a lease with the company, which occupies the building in return for rent. The lease provided by the company to the landlord is a covenant to pay an agreed rent over an agreed period. The period can be up to 25 years, but current market forces have reduced this to anything between five and 15 years. The obvious shortcoming of leasehold property is that the tenant may be responsible for substantial maintenance costs over the life of the lease and as a result, in the traditional developer/tenant relationship, there is little or no incentive for the developer to spend additional capital on construction to provide a low-maintenance building. This concept is reviewed in chapter 7, which deals with life cycle costing. Recently, a new concept of leasehold tenure has emerged, largely driven by public sector occupiers. This is a private finance initiative, referred to as a PFI scheme. Under the PFI funding route there is still a developer and the tenant is paying rent, but in an attempt to remove the cheap building but high maintenance problems of traditional landlord/tenant provision the landlord assumes responsibility for the maintenance of the building and the tenant pays an annual charge within the rent, which is calculated to amortise the maintenance costs over the lifetime of the lease. The clear benefit to both parties is that the building will be properly maintained, so preserving the landlord's investment, and the tenant can budget in advance, thus smoothing the peaks described in chapter 7 as the saw-tooth pattern of maintenance replacements. The increasing acceptance of facilities management as a professional service is reinforced by PFI schemes, whereby the management of the building throughout its lifetime by the landlord is not necessarily limited to maintenance of the fabric of the building but can also include the menu of non-core operational services described in chapter 5.

The new landlord does not buy the building for a price based on the development cost; it is an investment to the landlord and therefore the price paid to the company is valued as a function of the rental income that the investment will generate. Such valuations are subjective in that as an investor the landlord will seek a yield in percentage terms per annum and this percentage will vary according to the quality of the investment. Quality depends on the type of building concerned and its ability to be sold or relet on the open market in the event of the original occupier defaulting. The quality of the investment is also affected by the security of the occupier and therefore the security of the rental payments.

If it is desirable for the occupier of the building to retain complete control over design and construction, a 'develop, sale and leaseback' arrangement is appropriate. In this case the occupier funds the design and construction, then sells the investment to an institution while remaining in occupation as the sitting tenant.

The ideal solution in a develop, sale and leaseback deal is for the building to have wide market appeal and the tenant company to be viewed as blue chip security with regard to the rent. On the first point, for example, if the building is an institutional standard, high-bay warehouse adjacent to an international airport, then if it were to be vacated, it would not lie empty for long. On the second point, if the tenant is a publicly quoted, profitable company that is financially sound, then the rental payments will not be at risk. If satisfied these two points can turn a new building into a significant capital asset that could be sold at a substantial profit over the capital cost of its construction. The profit at the point of sale accrues to the occupier, who has acted as the developer and sold on the investment. The following example demonstrates the differences that can arise:

Capital cost of acquiring a site and developing a distribution warehouse, including finance charges:	£1 000 000
Open market rental value:	£160 000 p.a.
The develop and leaseback occupier is viewed as blue chip by the purchasing investor, who therefore figures a yield of:	8.5%

The yield percentage represents the annual return that the developer requires on the investment and is used to establish a multiplying factor applied to the rent to calculate the investment value. This is called the Years Purchase (YP) and is calculated by dividing 100 by the yield percentage. The better and more secure the investment, the lower the yield percentage and, as will become clear in the following example, the higher the purchase price of the investment. Vendors will therefore strive to negotiate the lowest possible yield, whereas the purchaser will wish to push the yield percentage upwards. Follow the next two comparative calculations as a demonstration of the effect of different covenants on first the yield and ultimately the realisable value of the investment.

In this example the YP is $100 \div 8.5 = 11.76$

The investment can now be valued at $£160\,000 \times 11.76 = £1\,881\,600$

The company receives £1.88 million in return for an outlay of £1 million and a rent agreement for £160 000 per annum.

Using the same development example, if the purchasing investor considers that the risk of the investment is higher he will require a shorter pay back period and may, for example, require a yield of 10.5%.

In this case the YP is $100 \div 10.5 = 9.52$ and the investment value is $£160\,000 \times 9.52 = £1.52$ million.

This is an indicative example, and because there are many other factors that affect yield in a free enterprise market, you must always seek the professional advice of a chartered surveyor experienced in the investment appraisal of your type of property.

The term for which a range of buildings will be retained within your portfolio will vary according to their function and any market pressures on the company. It is always prudent to consider this before acquisition and take the most appropriate view on how to acquire. In most cases purchase is a long-term ownership option and any property intended for short- or medium-term use is probably best leased with the possibility of extending the lease or shortening it as operational requirements dictate.

13.6 The Health and Safety file

The Construction (Design and Management) Regulations 1994 are binding on all new buildings and on many types of alteration and extension. Since their introduction in 1995 these regulations have required all building projects over a certain size to have a Health and Safety file which is held by the owner. This file must contain all the relevant facts about the building that have health and safety implications. This includes information on design, construction and potentially hazardous materials used in the construction. The file also deals with issues relating to the safe occupation and use of the building, plus all information relevant to the dismantling, alteration and eventual demolition of the building.

The Construction (Design and Management) Regulations 1994, issued by the Health and Safety Executive, details in appendix 5 the expected contents of the file.

Appendix 3 of the regulations sets out the parameters governing the application of the regulations to any construction project. As the facilities manager you are advised to seek professional help from a qualified planning supervisor when considering any construction project. The planning supervisor is a defined appointment under the regulations and is the expert who will ensure compliance for your project and also that it is the safest design possible for its intended use and life.

Generally, any construction project that involves more than a specified number of persons working on the site, or will exceed a defined duration or includes demolition work, falls under the regulations. At the moment these thresholds are low, but reference to the current edition of the regulations or a planning supervisor will determine the precise position.

Under these regulations the installation or replacement of process plant may also qualify as a notifiable project. Prior notification is a statutory requirement for all qualifying projects and must be lodged with the Health and Safety Executive before on-site work commences. There is a set pro forma for this notification.

Known hazards fall into two broad categories: those relating to the building itself, its design and use; and those arising from the processes being carried outside the building. If your building has the benefit of the Health and Safety File the first category will already be documented and you have an obligation to ensure that any changes to the building that materially affect health and safety are recorded in the file. With regard to the second category, it is very much the facilities manager's responsibility to ensure that proper consideration is given to the statutory requirements for health and safety at work. It is every employer's responsibility to ensure that persons on the employer's premises are not at risk. This is a requirement of the 1974 Health and Safety at Work Act and is all-embracing in its application. It applies to all persons on the premises, whether an employee or not. This does not mean that the facilities manager will carry out the safety assessments and write the safety policies, but he will need to ensure that these tasks are carried out by appropriately qualified personnel. These personnel can be internal safety officers or external consultants. Remember that failure to recognise or anticipate a hazard is no defence in court in the event of an accident.

Health and safety issues are dealt with in more detail in chapter 12.

13.7 Conclusion

The successful management of a property portfolio is both proactive and reactive, and the benefits will be greatest where proactive planning anticipates the changes to property requirements early enough to allow the slower response of adjustments to the portfolio to coincide with the timescale set by the operational requirements. New buildings, alterations and extensions are not an instant solution. They need to be designed, planned and constructed, and the process from inception to occupation, even with today's fast-track contracting methods, is seldom measured in less than months and large complex developments often take a year or more. The property portfolio is a major cost and therefore an overhead to the company. It must be managed with all the practical expertise the facilities manager can muster from his own experience, together with the advice of expert consultants and ultimately it must be commercially viable. The viability of the portfolio will be dictated by the strategic objectives set by the board and senior management, and the facilities manager will rely heavily on the company's finance director and accountant for direction on the question of viability. In enlightened organisations the facilities manager is increasingly being made responsible for overall portfolio management and coordinating the input of accountants and property consultants to arrive at the most effective solutions.

When the demand for portfolio change prevents a proactive approach, a reactive solution will be less efficient and a greater compromise because it will be driven by market availability. The terms for such a change will also be less favourable to the company as a buyer, because the initiative will move in favour of the seller. The task of the facilities manager is to generate as many options as possible when managing the existing and future portfolio.

Do not underestimate the value of objective professional help in property matters; good advice will always justify the fee because of the added value that it brings to the decision-making process and therefore to the value of the portfolio. Remember also that package-deal property providers – for example contractors who offer a turnkey contract to secure the site, develop the buildings and either sell or lease the building – are there to maximise their profits. Obtaining professional advice before entering into a contract can help prevent an expensive mistake that will burden the occupier with an inadequate building and expensive repair and reinstatement costs under the lease.

The latest developments in partnering and private finance initiatives contain a pointer to a possible solution. Under these arrangements the buildings acquired by a company, whether freehold or leasehold, from a developer or turnkey contractor can include a pre-agreed management element, whereby the provider is responsible for all maintenance and reinstatement costs throughout the lifetime of the building. This encourages better quality construction and the lifetime benefits of proper life cycle costing. These issues are discussed in chapter 7. On a cautionary note, remember that these solutions are new, and while they may appear effective, not enough time has passed to allow a significant number of projects to be completed and the expected success to be measured and confirmed from statistical feedback. It may take two rent review periods to confirm, in the case of PFI schemes, that the service charge levied on top of the commercial rent is equitable for both tenant and landlord.

14 Case Studies

14.1 Introduction

This chapter contains a selection of case studies, based on issues encountered by the author, that help to demonstrate the degreee of awareness expected from a facilities manager. It demonstrates the need for facilities managers to anticipate problems to be avoided as part of the preliminary planning process. In all the following case studies the facilities manager's involvement commenced early in the process and allowed good management practice of team problem solving, and in each example the facilities manager became the overall coordinator of the project. This is single point of contact management, which engenders ownership of the project and converts potential problems and delays into challenges that are overcome through the teamwork approach.

14.2 Study 1

The proposal

To construct a fuel distribution facility dispensing diesel to the company's delivery fleet. The chosen location is within the service yard of the fleet workshops.

The design

The project comprises a fuel island, a small administrative office and underground bulk storage. The fleet workshops are located next to a tidal estuary and geological investigation confirms that the site consists mainly of alluvial sand and silt with poor bearing capacity and a water table that fluctuates with tidal movement.

The facilities manager's interest

The project will be spearheaded by a technical design team and a contractor. The latter will be responsible for the performance of the facility for a period of twelve months beyond completion. This is the warranty period. The facilities manager remains responsible for fuel distribution for many years beyond the warranty period, and it could be argued that he has the greatest direct interest in the reliability of the operation. The particular problem with this project is that when the tide is out and the water table is low, if the storage tanks are full they will tend to sink as a result of their dead weight. The opposite will be true when the tide is in and the tanks are empty – they will float. In the latter case the storage tanks may push up the tarmac or concrete surfacing above.

These are extreme cases and the designers will make proper provisions to stabilise the tanks. In this case piles will be driven, a concrete slab cast to support the tanks and thus counter the sinking movement, and by strapping the tanks to the slab the floating effect will also be restrained.

This is not the end of the problem because, although the tanks will be restrained, there is still a risk of minor movement through settlement. Minor settlement would be enough to fracture the delivery pipework and create a pollution hazard, with the distinct possibility of diesel entering the tidal estuary.

A forward-thinking facilities manager will require confirmation from the designers that flexibility has been designed into the pipework and could also insist that a leak monitoring facility be added to the design. After all the operator of the fuel island will be responsible for any environmental matters associated with leakage and spillage. Potential contamination of the waterway will be monitored throughout the operational life of the island by enforcement bodies such as the Environment Agency, which will have the ultimate authority to close down the operation. Any responsible operator will actively avoid polluting the environment and it will be the task of the facilities manager to anticipate and eliminate as much of the risk as possible. Leak monitoring, regular inspections and a planned maintenance programme are all proactive measures that reduce the probability of a discharge. There is, however, no such thing as an entirely foolproof solution and so, in addition to the planned safeguards, the facilities manager must include emergency procedures to contain or minimise the damage in the event of an accident or component failure.

Responsibility for any failure that can be attributed to negligence on the part of a designer, whether a consultant or one engaged by a design and build contractor, extends for many years beyond the contract warranty period. The precise period will be defined in the contract, and in the construction industry the norm is 12 years. The facilities manager should ensure that professional indemnity insurance covering all events arising from negligent design is in place at the time when the design is being carried out and that it is a contractual requirement for the same level of cover to be maintained for the full period of responsibility. If there is concern that the design consultant or the contractor may not remain in business for the full term, the facilities manager would be well advised to consider a stand-alone indemnity insurance policy written in favour of the facilities manager's company.

14.3 Study 2

The proposal

To install new blast-freezing equipment in an existing cold storage and distribution centre. The cold store is a portal-framed industrial building with a secondary insulated box inside, supported by the portal frames. The freezing equipment is located within the void space above the insulated ceiling and under the roof of the building.

The facilities manager's interest

The new equipment can be easily installed by crane from the service yard, once the roof panels above the installation location are temporarily removed. The facilities manager is charged with the task of keeping the cold store operational throughout and staff will continue to drive forklift trucks within the chilled areas. In order to ensure the safety of the staff the facilities manager must coordinate the equipment-lifting operations and staff access to the cold store, so that if the new plant is accidentally dropped by the crane and breaks through to the chilled areas there will be no risk of injury or fatality. This is an obvious hazard that, under the Construction (Design and Management) Regulations introduced in 1995, will be addressed by the statutory project health and safety plan and it places defined responsibilities on both the designers and the principal contractor. These responsibilities are dealt with in chapter 12.

There is a less obvious operational hazard that concerns the operation of the cold store. The top of the insulated box is not waterproof and any rain entering through the access hole in the roof will collect as a puddle on top of the box and permeate through. The water will fall on the floor of the cold store and freeze in an area where warehouse staff are picking up loads from high-bay racking using forklift trucks. This potentially catastrophic hazard could easily result in serious injury or even death, and almost certainly in prosecution by the Health and Safety Executive.

14.4 Study 3

The proposal

To consider whether or not outside factors or land uses beyond the boundary of the premises have an effect on the operation of the facilities. The granting of planning consent and building regulation approval is not a categorical confirmation that the facilities manager's proposed use is compatible with the existing activities of the adjoining premises. This is another issue that is reinforced by the Construction (Design and Management) Regulations, which formalise the requirement to establish and review adjoining occupations.

The example

Consider a distribution warehouse operating as a collection point for courier services. The warehouse is situated immediately adjacent to a commercial airport as the operation is based on worldwide express delivery and air freight is the chosen transportation method.

The facilities manager's interests

There are the obvious factors of noise from the airport, lighting restrictions imposed by the airport authorities and, if vehicle movements in and out of the distribution centre are intensive, any restrictions imposed by emergency procedures at the airport.

There are also a number of less obvious restrictions that will impact on the operation of the warehouse. Jet engines are particularly susceptible to damage from debris and airport authorities are acutely sensitive to discarded packaging material that can be blown by the wind out of the service yards onto the aprons or runways. Foreign object damage (FOD) avoidance is critical during take off and landing, so proper provision and good housekeeping in running a tidy operation with enclosed refuse disposal will almost certainly be a requirement. If the warehouse is under the approach flightpath there will be further restrictions on maintenance work on the roof, and detailed specifications may be applied to the fixing system for the roof decking.

The facilities manager will be expected to control all these factors effectively without placing excessive restrictions on the commercial operation of the warehouse.

14.5 Study 4

The proposal

To consider the installation of plant and process equipment in an existing building.

The design

The health and safety issues surrounding the installation of plant is now governed in many cases by the Construction (Design and Management) Regulations in that fixed plant must conform to the regulations and be sited so that it can be installed, maintained and subsequently removed with the minimum of risk.

The facilities manager's interests

This invariably means siting plant where it can be mechanically placed in position or removed: it is always better to handle heavy items mechanically and avoid manual handling operations. Whenever possible plan easy access for cranes, delivery vehicles or forklift trucks. If major pieces of plant, for example boilers, heat exchangers or air handling units, can be sited next to the perimeter fabric of a building with access from outside through demountable panels, this will address the safety issue. The payback comes through increased efficiency of installation, maintenance and removal, together with separating these activities from the operations within the building.

There are particular safety issues to address when installing process plant, and included in the Construction (Design and Management) Regulations is the risk of operatives falling from a height of 2 metres or more. If, during installation, maintenance or removal, operatives will be working 2 metres or more above the ground, reference to these regulations is necessary.

14.6 Study 5

The proposal

A 1970s office block is about to be modernised by an owner-occupier who wishes to install furnishings and equipment.

The design

The new equipment presents some structural problems in that the floor loadings will be increased to a level that could become dangerous to the structure. In addition the heat gain from the new equipment will necessitate an element of air handling and comfort control.

The facilities manager's interests

Initial appraisal suggested that the scheme could not be carried out without excessively compromising comfort. The existing storey height was insufficient to accommodate cable servicing to the equipment and the air distribution ductwork. The eventual solution entailed removal of the existing floor screeds and a replanned workstation layout that avoided the need for a raised access floor. The screed removal reduced the dead load on the structure sufficiently to safeguard its structural integrity and created additional storey height to allow installation of the air distribution ductwork. In this example the occupier succeeded in modernising the workspace, the only compromise being the loss of workstation layout flexibility that occurred when the access floors were abandoned. The facilities manager in this case minimised the impact of this compromise through his knowledge of the operating activities of the building and achieving the optimum working layout from the outset.

14.7 Study 6

The proposal

To install new pressure vessels and pipework within an existing operational building.

The design

The certification, testing and insurance requirements governing the new pressure vessels and pipework prohibited flanged joints and stipulated that only welded joints would be acceptable. The location of the installation prevented prefabrication and dictated assembly and welding on site. The location of the installation was within the battery charging area of the fleet of forklift trucks.

The facilities manager's interests

The facilities manager was presented with an apparently impossible situation: spark-generating welding work in an atmosphere that was potentially heavy with hydrogen from the battery charging. Air quality tests suggested a definite risk of explosion.

The facilities manager consulted a health and safety planning supervisor who, in conjunction with the contractor and the Health and Safety Executive inspector, devised a safe method of work. A temporary, airtight cocoon was constructed around the welding area and positive air pressure was provided in the enclosure by fans ducted from the open air. This ensured that any air leakage would move outwards from the working area into the charging area, making it impossible for any excess hydrogen to enter the hot working area.

14.8 Commentary

Many of these case studies draw from examples prompted by increased safety awareness and the statutory requirements imposed on construction-related work since 1995. It is now a fundamental requirement when designing and constructing buildings to give due consideration to their lifetime safety, so it is vital that facilities managers are aware of these responsibilities. Responsibility is not vested solely in the facilities manager but is placed in clearly defined terms upon clients (the building owner and on occasion the occupier if different), designers and contractors. The facilities manager must ensure that all members of the team fulfil their individual responsibilities, otherwise he will risk assuming complete liability, by default, even for those disciplines where he is neither experienced nor qualified. The final case study in this chapter is again taken from an actual project and demonstrates that the final solution to a safety problem need not be expensive.

14.9 Study 7

The proposal

To consider the maintenance requirements and method of working for a new distribution warehouse.

The facilities manager's interests

The project designers responsible for the new warehouse identified through their statutory risk assessments that a genuine hazard would exist if casual access to the roof was possible. Maintenance and operational reasons dictated that access to the roof would be by a fixed metal access platform and ladder. This is the warehouse on the perimeter of the airport described in Study 3, and the roof would be attractive as an unauthorised viewing point into the airport. Simply designating the roof as out of bounds would be insufficient as a safety measure, and if unauthorised access was easy and someone fell off the roof accidentally, the building owner would undoubtedly be prosecuted by the Health and Safety Executive. If the accident was fatal or permanently disabling the penalties from a successful prosecution would be severe.

The designers proposed that guard rails be fitted to the roof, but this would be excessively expensive and would interfere with the watertight integrity of the roof decking. The proposal was reviewed as part of the project value engineering exercise and the final solution was to move the access platform and fixed ladder inside the building and control access to the bottom section of the ladder by a locked mesh cage. Only authorised personnel would have a key and all would be trained in safe working methods, using harness restraints on the roof, and fully versed in control of materials likely to generate debris. The guard rails were not installed.

14.10 Conclusion

In building, property management and facilities management, the problems encountered are often unique to each project or building, so the facilities manager is well advised to develop an ability to think laterally and anticipate less obvious events. Always seek input from other team members and interested parties with beneficial contributions to make to the management process. Avoid the excessive haste that seems to be increasingly common in the desire for fast track procurement. Remember that taking a little longer over the preplanning of a project in order to maximise accident prevention is always preferable to recourse to claims, litigation and insurance. When viewed in retrospect the measured approach invariably proves to be the best commercial solution.

Recommended Further Reading and References

CIOB Handbook of Facilities Management, ed. Alan Spedding, 1994, published by Longman Scientific & Technical

Facilities Management: Theory and Practice, Keith Alexander, 1996, published by E & F. N. Spon

References

Construction (Design and Management) Regulations 1994 and Approved Code of Practice, published by the Health and Safety Executive

Designing for Health and Safety in Construction, published by the Health and Safety Executive

A Guide to Managing Health and Safety in Construction, published by the Health and Safety Executive

Health and Safety in Construction, published by the Health and Safety Executive

CIOB Construction Information File — Construction Papers series, published by the Chartered Institute of Building

Index